To Life

A Guide to Finding Your Path Back to Health

Teresa Tsalaky

To Life
Publications

P.O. Box 157
Crescent City, CA 95531
www.tolifeonline.com

Retta — May your angels always be with you. Hugs, — Anne Prechen artist

Retta, Health and Joy to you in abundance
Teresa Tsalaky

Cover art and book design by Annie Wilkin, Creative Ink

Printed in the United States of America

Passages from THE TURNING POINT by Fritjof Capra reprinted with the permission of Simon & Schuster. Copyright © 1981 by Fritjof Capra.

Publisher's Cataloging-in-Publication

Tsalaky, Teresa.
    To Life : a guide to finding your path back to health
    / Teresa Tsalaky. -- 1st ed.
        p. cm.
    Includes bibliographical references and index.
     ISBN 0-97218-940-8

    1. Alternative medicine. 2. Mind and body--Health
aspects. 3. Self-care, Health.   I. Title.

R733.T73 2002   615.5
                    QBI33-612

If you are unable to order this book from your local bookseller,
you may order directly from the publisher.
Quantity discounts are available.

To Life Publications
P.O. Box 157, Crescent City, CA 95531
707-465-1032
www.tolifeonline.com

Disclaimer: The purpose of this book is to encourage readers to take responsibility for their health and healing. It does not prescribe medical treatment or dispense medical advice. It recommends you work with a health-care practitioner while working to heal yourself. The author, publisher, distributor, or those whose names appear in this book shall have no liability or responsibility for any loss or damage caused (or allegedly caused) by the information presented in this book. What you choose to do with this and all health-related information is your responsibility. Accepting that responsibility is a key to healing.

Acknowledgements

Loving gratitude to:
   Dr. Glenna Wilde, who empowers her patients.
   Clinton Ray Miller, who fights the good fight.
   Claudia Frances, for keeping the faith and the files.
   Lynne Rackley, a well of wisdom.
   Dr. Stewart DeVault, for sharing his knowledge.
   Susan Rossiter, for eleventh-hour proofing.
   The late Dr. Roy Barnes, a healing genius.
   The Coalition for Natural Health, for getting the word out.
   John and Molly Tsalaky, for paying for journalism school.
   The self-healers who shared their stories.
   Annie Wilkin, who inspired it all.

Contents

Section Two: Breaking Through the Illusions

Section Three: The Path Back to Health

To Life

A Guide to Finding Your Path Back to Health

Foreword

My first thought when I started to read this book was, "Thank God for the First Amendment." This is precisely the kind of book that would be on top of the list to be burned in any country with a medical monopoly.

I like this book. I really like it. It attacks a mindset that is keeping millions of us sick and unhappy or living far below that level of health that we should be enjoying. But it attacks so gently that I was unaware it was changing my thinking until I did something I had procrastinated doing for sixty-five years. This book has already changed my life for the better, and I didn't even have any of the serious medical problems it tells about in the twenty unbelievable stories of self-healing.

I call them unbelievable because they are. Just because they are true doesn't make them more believable to most of us.

Try this experiment on your sickest friends and your medical doctor: Loan them the book and ask them to read about the self-healers. It is fascinating to see the reaction of sick people and medical doctors who believe incurable people should not rock their belief system by healing themselves. Most people and most medical doctors really believe that diseases labeled "incurable" are incurable.

To those of us with direct experience in self-healing, the stories are believable. But this book is not just a book of true stories—believable or not. It is also a book that shatters two major illusions. What is amazing is that Teresa shatters these two illusions without a sledgehammer. She does it with a feather quill pen. When I attack these illusions, it goes something like this: "@%^&!~#*+/<!>#@!!" Teresa, on the other hand, does not use a single unkind word.

Once an illusion is shattered, like Humpty Dumpty, all the king's horses and all the king's men cannot put it together again. If you do not want to be dis-illusioned, skip over Section Two, "Breaking Through the Illusions."

Don't worry. The testimonials alone are worth ten times the price of the book.

I'm a testimonial junkie. I thrive on them. Even when it takes a person an entire book to write his testimonial, I love to read it. So, to find twenty accounts of self-healing so well written in a single book was, well, unbelievable.

I probably would have found it difficult to believe the tale of Tricia Bies—whose tumor plopped out on the floor—if I had not had several similar experiences on a much smaller (thankfully) scale.

I have had skin cancer for the past thirty years. I am now eighty and have spent the last fifty years as a health-freedom legislative advocate on a federal and state level.

As a young boy sixty-five years ago, it was considered neat to have a deep tan at the end of every summer. I spent every minute I could in the sun. No sunscreen. No warning. Just cute girls who flattered me for my gorgeous tan.

Twenty-five years later, the skin cancers started appearing on my nose, ear and shoulder. At first, the one on my nose was about the size of a small pea. As it grew, my friends encouraged me to go to the Hoxsey clinic in Mexico. They said Hoxsey had a salve that would "pull it out." I wasn't at all concerned, because I was on a good diet—lots of vitamins and minerals—and surrounded by a host of alternative doctors who were curing cancer. I was surprised that they all recommended I have it cut off.

Finally, at the insistence of my boss and another friend, I went to the cancer clinic in Mexico. A nurse put some bloodroot salve on the tumor and warned me, "Now, this will really hurt."

It did. I mean hurt. And my tumor was miniscule.

I can't imagine the pain a woman suffers who has a large breast tumor like that of Tricia Bies.

But when it came out (mine didn't plop on the floor), it had come out roots and all. I had felt excruciating pain several inches away from the tumor. The roots were deep. Over several years, other tumors on my shoulder and ear were treated in like manner, and the cancers came out clean—it seemed with far less pain each time, perhaps because I knew what to expect. I would never hesitate to use bloodroot salve because of the pain.

The friend who went with me to Hoxsey had a cancer on his forehead. He had gone to a surgeon to have it cut off when it was the size of a bean. The surgeon said, "I think we got it all." He hadn't. It came back the size of a dime. He went to the same surgeon again, who cut it off again and assured my friend that, "I'm sure we got it all this time." He hadn't. It came back the size of a quarter. Ditto. Ditto. It came back the size of a silver dollar. That's when he finally decided to go to Hoxsey.

Because of my unbelievable experience, I couldn't understand why every doctor would not quickly believe me and at least offer the salve as an alternative with a warning that it would be really painful. I talked to many doctors. They all yawned.

Would I encourage people to use bloodroot, poke root and other escharotics to pull out cancers instead of cutting (part of) them out? In a heartbeat. And I would do all in my power to encourage every reader of this book to become a self-healer, no matter how serious or "incurable" your condition.

Become a self-healer.

Go forward.

— **Clinton Ray Miller**

Preface

This book began with one premise: If you have a chronic illness, your best hope of finding a cure is to take responsibility for your own healing.

It was written using these precepts:

• It's okay to begin with a premise, but follow the story wherever it leads. In the search for truth, you must be willing to alter or even abandon your initial premise.

• Experience elucidates truth, so tell the story from the perspective of people who have lived it.

And so I went looking for people who had lived it. I sent a notice to newsletters saying I was looking for people who had chronic illnesses and refused to stop looking for a cure until they found one. I interviewed all who called or to whom I was referred. Their illnesses covered a wide range of so-called "incurables," including malignant cancers, diabetes, lupus, multiple sclerosis, Crohn's disease, fibromyalgia, shingles, chronic fatigue syndrome, arrhythmia, asthma and systemic candida. Most had found cures. This was no surprise.

But their stories led to unexpected conclusions.

The first was that the healing journey has a set of common factors. For example, most of the self-healers in this book did not take responsibility for their health until they were sick enough to reach the end of their emotional ropes. And almost all who then took the healing journey were transformed by it. Many were affected so profoundly that they changed their professions in order to help others heal. Others went through emotional or spiritual transformations. I was surprised by the number who cured themselves by diet changes alone. And I was dismayed by the number who attributed their illnesses at least partly to common dental practices—dismayed because there are three dentists in my family.

Their stories led to in-depth research to understand why they had to find their cures outside of the doctor's office and why so few people look there. Why do 100 million Americans have illnesses labeled "chronic"—

15

in other words, illnesses that neither doctor nor patient knows how to cure?

You will read stories of people who suffered for years at the hands of a medical system often unable to correctly diagnose or effectively cure. Then you will read about the roots of allopathy (the type of medicine practiced by medical doctors) and the forces that shaped it while it grew to dominate health care in the United States. I think you'll conclude that the sorry state of American medicine is not the doctors' fault. These physicians know their diagnostic manuals. They follow established treatment protocols. They act in accordance with their profession's standards. They want to help their patients. They are simply locked into a system that rarely allows for healing.

One of the stories you'll read is about a woman named Tricia Bies who has been treating her cancer using various alternative methods. A year after our initial interview, I called her for an update. Tired of the struggle, she had decided to give some of the responsibility for her healing back to the doctors. She chose to take chemotherapy. "I thought I'd be kicked out of the book," she said.

But my journalism training runs deep, and I could not exclude something just because it seemed to contradict the book's premise. In fact, that part of Tricia's story adds a valuable understanding of the healing path: Even if you accept responsibility for your own healing, there may be a time when it's wise to go back to the doctor and include his medicine. And so my initial premise was not abandoned but had to be widened to accommodate a wider range of experience.

Just before publication, Tricia's tumors were once again shrinking. My sincere hope is that her story and the struggles and triumphs of the other self-healers in this book give you the courage to take the healing path.

— **Teresa Tsalaky**

16

MEET THE SELF-HEALERS

When disease emerges
Accept, embrace, listen, respond.
Receive the blessing of those who suffer;
They are the heroes
Who show us the divine in ourselves.
—The Tao of Healing,
adapted from the Tao Te Ching

Chapter 1

The Heroes of Healing

You are about to meet twenty self-healers. They encountered diseases ranging from cancer to candidiasis, from diabetes to lupus, from asthma to AIDS. Many are completely healed. A few remain on the healing journey. Some used only natural methods to become well. Others used a combination of allopathy and its alternatives. They each chose a different healing path. But they all share one thing in common: At some point, they made a decision to take responsibility for their health. And that decision was the turning point—the place where hopelessness turned into hope, where powerlessness turned into empowerment, where the incurable became curable.

It is the purpose of this book to encourage you to make that decision to take responsibility for your health. Untold thousands of sick and suffering people have done so. The twenty you'll read about are simply a sampling. Their stories are meant to give you hope that you, too, may heal if you will take responsibility for doing so.

In this book, you'll learn of their tragedies and triumphs, their fears and failures, the treatments that worked and the treatments that didn't. You'll see how their health problems brought them to the end of hope and how they didn't give up; how they found the courage to step beyond our cultural conditioning and try something different; how they stared down death and disease, mustering the perseverance to keep trying another practitioner, another treatment, another change in lifestyle; how they became transformed on the path back to health; and how they are now living that transformed life.

They each took a hero's journey.

19

Mythologist Joseph Campbell describes the hero's journey not as the conquest of a warrior or the life-saving actions of a fireman but rather as the inner journey of an ordinary man who, through his trials, develops the courage and wisdom to triumph.

So this is a book about people transformed into heroes—people who did, in fact, save a life: their own. It's not only about people who got well, but also about people who reclaimed their power, taking it back from the hands of the medical gods we call doctors and using it to heal. Their stories are meant to prompt you to take the first step on your hero's journey.

This book is for you if you're sick and tired of being sick and tired; if your intuition tells you there's more you could do to heal; if you're simply curious about alternatives to drugs and surgery; if you have a chronic condition that won't go away; if the doctor has said, 'There's nothing more we can do,' or 'There is no cure;' if you're at the end of your rope and need some hope; if you've been given a medical death sentence and want to live; or if you simply want to avoid another operation, another drug, another set of side effects.

In Section One of this book, you will read how some of the self-healers came to the end of their ropes, how their illnesses developed into debilitating or life-threatening diseases, and how they suffered and struggled not knowing where to turn for help.

Section Two is devoted solely to breaking through the two illusions that keep us sick: the illusion that we're not responsible for our health and the illusion that the doctor's medicine is best. It's full of statistics, scientific study results and the observations of experts, because these things have a way of breaking through illusions. No matter how convincing the stories of the self-healers in this book, they will not motivate you to act unless you have begun to see through these two illusions—or at least to consider that they might be illusions and begin testing them yourself in search of your own truth.

In Section Three, you'll find out how the self-healers resolved their diseases, what treatments they used, what spiritual, emotional and physical methods led to healing.

Their stories are intensely personal. In them, they share some of their deepest fears. Because their healing methods are not all mainstream, they may be exposing themselves to the judgment of others. But each had a reason to take the risk. Some believe their stories point to a larger truth. Some want to give hope to people who are sick and feel stuck without options. Here's how Jacquelyn Compton, who you will meet in the next chapter, explains why she was willing to tell the intimate story of her disease and healing:

"The storyteller in this country's western Native American culture is depicted as an open-mouthed seated figure upon whose lap and around the feet are many smaller figures. This symbol has become a challenge and a beacon to me. The tradition of telling of the experiences of those who have gone before validates our existence. Like a map, it reminds us of who we are and where we have been. I believe it is in the telling of stories we equip our future generations to live meaningful lives. It is in telling my story that I am able to see a door that is otherwise imperceptible. It is in going through the door that I affirm who I am. It is on the other side of that door I become who I shall be."

Chapter 2

Jacquelyn Compton

When the doctor pronounced Jacquelyn Compton's death sentence, he didn't look at her. Instead, he talked directly to her husband. "He was concerned with the person who was going to go on living," Jacquie says.

She had undergone five operations in thirteen months. At age twenty-six, she had given birth to her fourth child, and at the post-birth checkup, the doctor could tell something remained in the uterus. This was 1968, before sonograms were available as a window inside the uterus. The doctor performed a dilation and curettage, scraping out the walls of the uterus. "This monstrous thing began to emerge. It was larger than a grapefruit," Jacquie recalls.

It was cancerous, so surgeons removed the uterus. Soon thereafter, they operated again to repair Jacquie's bladder. She remained in pain, so they cut her open yet again to remove her ovaries and fallopian tubes. Her body began amassing scar tissue "to defend itself," Jacquie says. "The intestines were bound up in this adhesion material. They tried to strip off this adhesion stuff in another operation; they laid my entire intestines on the table. Now I'd had five operations, and I still had polyps in the bladder."

The doctor told Jacquie's husband that Jacquie would live two more years at most. "He said there was nothing more they could do. He said, 'Go inland where it's warm and dry, and take your wife, because she isn't going to be around long.'"

Doctors may have considered Jacquie already dead, but Jacquie's emotions at hearing the news were very much alive.

"I had a feeling of, 'Oh, no. I'm not ready.' I come from a Swedish background, and they're very task oriented. The one thing worse than being a liar is being lazy. So I thought, 'Oh my goodness, I mustn't be untidy about this; I have to get things taken care of.'"

Setting her affairs in order meant preparing her four young children for her departure.

"My kids were aware I was terribly ill, because life was so chaotic. I don't think children understand die. I think they just understand Mom goes away. I told them I could go away, and I was going to make sure everything was going to be taken care of."

But Mom didn't go away.

"For those of us who grew up on novels where the heroine lays down and dies, I thought, 'Well, I think I'll just lay down and die.' So you lay down, then the phone rings, or one of your children calls for you, or the neighbor stops by, and you just don't die."

Jacquie just kept living. She changed her diet and took care of her soul. And she continued living. During the next twenty-five years, she didn't make a single trip to the doctor's office.

Chapter 3

Linda Koep

L inda Koep was an active mother of two teen-age boys when her world began falling apart. She worked a full-time job and stayed in shape by walking, lifting weights and mountain biking.

In 1989, she began experiencing strange, subtle sensations. When she exercised, she felt pressure in her head, followed by weakness and dizziness. A ringing phone would give her a chill and create a flash of anxiety.

Her doctor said, "There are so many bugs going around right now, let's give you antibiotics," Linda recalls. He did blood work and a test for Lyme disease—a tick-borne infection—but found nothing. Her blood pressure was fine.

But the symptoms persisted. So she went back to the doctor a couple weeks after the initial visit. "He said, 'That's really a nasty bug. Let's give it another round of antibiotics,'" Linda recalls.

Soon afterward, the symptoms progressed to aching joints, skin rashes, diarrhea and unusual feelings difficult to describe. Some were strange and scary. Linda recalls one particularly disconcerting experience at work: "After having some Christmas treats with coworkers, I was sitting at my desk. As I stood to reach something, I felt like I could hear and see everything going on around me, but I couldn't speak and felt numb. I fell into my chair and couldn't even call out. It seemed like hours, but it was probably only a minute or two. A coworker noticed I looked strange, and she said something, but I couldn't respond."

Linda went back to the doctor. He checked her blood sugar, and it was low but still within normal range. He decided she had an inner ear infection and suggested more antibiotics. She took them and got worse.

So she began looking for culprits. She examined all the events in her life leading up to the symptoms. They had begun soon after she'd had a root canal, so she talked to her dentist about her symptoms. He assured her the root canal procedure was not the culprit

Linda decided to try another doctor, then another, then another. She went to a general practitioner, an internist, a neurologist. Each new doctor had a new diagnosis and a different prescription.

Linda was suffering from a modern-day illness that has become common due to the overuse of antibiotics. The allopathic community is reluctant to recognize diseases caused by its own practices, so Linda's doctors did not understand her strange symptoms.

One symptom, for example, was "a dizzy, disconnected, swimmy feeling in my back," Linda recalls. "My back felt sick. But the doctors would say, 'How can you be dizzy in your back?' They totally disregarded that as being possible."

One doctor decided the spinal discomfort meant the start of multiple sclerosis—a disease in which spinal cord tissue can harden and cause muscle tremors and paralysis. Linda panicked. "I had seen people with MS wither away and die, and at this point, I was withering away." She also had a frequent sensation of being about to lose consciousness, and she occasionally did black out.

Linda went to the library and started reading about MS. What she read did not match her experience, but she had no other explanation for her medley of symptoms.

"If I had MS, I thought there must be some diagnostic test. I wanted a definite answer so that I could do something." But the tests came back inconclusive. Other doctors agreed her symptoms were similar to MS symptoms and said they couldn't rule it out.

By now, Linda had been diagnosed and un-diagnosed with a bacterial infection, a virus, an inner ear infection, pinched nerves, sinusitis, Lyme disease and MS. She had been hospitalized twice. Numerous MDs had listened to her symptoms and used all the high-tech gadgets at their disposal. They took x-rays, drew blood, did CAT scans, an MRI imaging test, a spinal tap, a myelogram, an echocardiogram and several electro-cardiograms. They prescribed antibiotics, painkillers and tranquilizers.

But they still had no cure. They didn't even know what was wrong with her.

"So I got labeled a mental health case," Linda says in her gentle, lilting voice. A family member had suffered depression, and that was all the doctors needed to know to get themselves off the hook.

They sent Linda to a psychiatrist.

"The psychiatrist put a clock in front of me and said we had twenty minutes. Then he talked for twenty minutes about how I was creating my symptoms. He didn't ask if I was experiencing stress or what was going on in my life. He had made his decision before I even got there," Linda recalls. "I had always heard that people who are crazy are the last to know, so I was open to the possibility. But after a few appointments, I asked, 'If you're telling me I'm creating this dizziness by hyperventilating, when are you going to teach me to breathe correctly?'"

The psychiatrist prescribed antidepressants—four in all. They made Linda anxious, and for five weeks she did not sleep, adding insomnia to her symptoms.

"At this point, I was really losing myself. The drugs were changing my brain chemistry. I was reduced to staying in my house, because the panic and anxiety were so bad because of the chemical imbalance. On days that the anxiety was particularly acute, I would pace back and forth, trying to keep myself busy with anything I could. I felt like a caged animal. It was terrifying. My family was sick with worry."

Her mother and sister came to visit. They cried all the way home.

Linda, once athletic and strong, had lost nearly a quarter of her body weight. At five-foot-ten, she was down to one hundred and twelve pounds.

Linda has been well now for more than ten years. She now knows what was wrong with her and what cured it. Her illness was caused by two common allopathic practices. A combination of four natural substances cured her. The Food and Drug Administration will close down any business that touts this combination as an effective cure.

Chapter 4

Andrew Yachad

Several times during his childhood, Andrew Yachad thought he was going to die. Any physical activity beyond walking would cause his lungs to stop working. While fighting the sensation of suffocating, he would reach for his asthma inhaler, but he'd be so weak from lack of oxygen, his fingers wouldn't work. He had to put a capsule into the inhaler, which had two needles in its cap that punctured the capsule before it could be inhaled. Andrew lived in South Africa, and his family had a maid. He believes he would have died had she not been there many times to prepare the inhaler when he could not.

The doctor had diagnosed grass and pollen allergies. It wasn't the only lung-related problem. Almost every winter, Andrew came down with bronchitis. Twice he had to be hospitalized. For a young boy, being unable to play sports was frustrating.

"At age fourteen, I was tired of living like this," Andrew said.

He recalls asking the doctor what could be done. The doctor said his condition was incurable. But Andrew wasn't going to give up to his illness so easily. He went to the library and started doing his own research.

Within six months, he was playing soccer. Twenty-five years later, he keeps his inhaler handy only for the very rare occasion when he unwittingly eats something that brings on an attack.

Chapter 5

Sharon Rosa

On July 27, 1993, Sharon Rosa was pronounced dead. She floated out of her body. She saw a man with teal-blue eyes approaching her and knew his name was Jeremy.

"His eyes just sang. He didn't speak, he just radiated through his eyes," Sharon recalls. The man took her to a room with a podium and began throwing books at her—ancient medical texts. "I read them so fast. I thought, 'This is hurting my head.' He's beaming at me with great pleasure." Then her grandfather, who had also died on a July 27, told Sharon she had to go back. "I woke up filled with so much knowledge, it was giving me a headache," Sharon recalls.

It was the first of two near-death experiences brought about by her disease.[1]

Sharon had experienced health problems her entire life, suffering bouts of diarrhea and vomiting as a child. She was treated for asthma and chronic fatigue. At other times, doctors said there was nothing wrong with her. In spite of ongoing illness, she made it through high school and college, earning a degree in finance and marketing.

Sharon excelled rapidly in the business world. By age twenty-seven, she was overseeing her company's United States division in corporate banking. She sometimes had high fevers, but she was enjoying her job, traveling a lot and pleased with her life.

Then one day in 1989, while sitting in an airport waiting for a flight, she lost control of her bladder.

"I was in bed for the next eighteen months, and the only thing that was working was my brain." She was diagnosed with two incurable diseases:

31

multiple sclerosis and antiphospholipid syndrome—a severe form of lupus.

Two years after diagnosis, she began having seizures. When her disease was at its worst, Sharon spent three weeks in the hospital unaware that she was there. Her weight dropped to eighty-two pounds. The seizures increased in frequency to as many as thirty-six a day. And finally, her body gave out.

That's when she had the first of two near-death experiences that put her on the road to a new profession in medicine.

The second time she died, Jeremy met her again and took her to a council of medicine men. Each gave her an item or information. "The Indian man gave me a bag of herbs. The other guy was from Roman or Greek times and prepared me for new diseases and gave me more information about the brain, seizures and the immune system. I was told that I'd be mocked and ridiculed, but persevere, we'll be with you."

Sharon woke up in the hospital wearing a diaper and with electrodes covering her head. And she decided to become a doctor.

Today, she is a naturopathic physician. Her practice is called Awakenings—named after the movie starring Robin Williams as a doctor who finds a way to bring a patient out of a catatonic state.

"I know what it's like to take your last breath. I know what it's like to be on both sides of the desk (as doctor and patient). I went through being misdiagnosed all my life; I was injected with drugs that made me sicker. I believe I chose my illness to get into health care."

In fact, she believes all chronically ill people can find meaning in their illness.

"If we don't listen to our higher self—God, spirit, whatever you call it —to tap into our soul, our body is going to tell us with pain or illness to make us listen to that little small voice that people don't want to listen to," she said. "I want people to know there is a higher power, an inner divine intelligence, and illness serves a purpose."

Chapter 6

Darla Greenig

Darla Greenig came from a family of ten children. The family had an unspoken rule about health. "The rule was you don't get ill. If you do get ill, you don't show it," Darla recalls. So when Darla began getting tired and sore at age thirty-nine, she followed the rules. "I continued the code by doing as well as I could and not complaining." She began drinking guarana for energy and taking pills to sleep. But the tiredness and muscle aches and insomnia never went away. They slowly got worse.

"There were times when I hurt so much all over, there was not a place on my entire body where I could have put a silver dollar and it wouldn't have touched a sore spot," Darla recalls. At times, she felt confused and depressed. But she continued to follow the family code, hiding her illness from her husband and children by never complaining. "I disguised it as well as I could, so my family didn't say, 'Go to the doctor.'"

After fifteen years, Darla was still suffering. She still didn't know what caused her symptoms or what might cure them. Finally, one day, she told a friend about her pain and fatigue. The friend sent her a packet of information about fibromyalgia. In it, she read that fibromyalgia simply means pain in the fibrous tissues of the body—the muscles, tendons and ligaments—and that the symptoms consist of fatigue and aching all over. "I read it and I just wept, because there was a name to all this craziness I was going through."

She went to a rheumatologist who confirmed the self-diagnosis and said the disease had no known cause or cure. He could do nothing more than prescribe pain medication.

That wasn't good enough for Darla. She decided to take matters into her own hands.

Over the last six years, Darla has taken the long, slow climb back toward health. "I'm eighty percent better," she says. "Yes, I do still have pain, but it's not overwhelming. I can now put in five hours of moderate work in my garden or house. Five years ago, it was half an hour. I'll reach one-hundred percent someday."

Chapter 7

Sarah Clemente

Sarah Clemente, age fourteen, has a message for anyone who will listen: "I want people to know that they don't have to be sick. They don't have to feel bad," she says. "There's a different way that's so much easier than taking the medicine. That sums it up."

Sarah's healing journey began at age twelve when her vision began to diminish. An eye exam before the start of the school year showed no vision problems. A month later, Sarah could no longer see words on the chalkboard at the front of the classroom. A new exam showed 20/200 vision in one eye and that Sarah had developed cataracts. Children's Hospital provided the diagnosis: Type 1 diabetes.

Also known as juvenile diabetes, this is a condition in which the pancreas produces little or no insulin. Sarah was soon giving herself insulin shots twice a day, a total of forty-one units. "The shots were awful," Sarah recalls. The doctors said she'd have to take insulin the rest of her life. It was a hereditary disease, and she was stuck with it, they said.

But Sarah's mother, Sue, had been through her own healing journey, and she knew that the body has tremendous healing power if it is given the proper support. She told Sarah there may be a way to control the diabetes without the regular shots. Mother and daughter devised a self-treatment that both could do together. And today, Sarah takes insulin only when she gets the flu or on holidays when she eats too many raw-food sweets.

"There are so many people out there who don't have to go through shots," Sarah says. "I just wish people knew that."

Chapter 8

Madhuri Cawley

Madhuri Cawley's life had prepared her to deal with illness at all three levels: body, mind and spirit.

When she was eleven, her father died, and she responded by developing a strong spirituality that she says has been the foundation of her life ever since. Her first college degree was in psychology, providing her with an understanding of the mental and emotional aspects of illness. Her second degree led to work as a physician's assistant, and she later attended pre-med, aspiring to medical school but becoming too physically ill to complete the program. She also studied several alternative therapies, including polarity therapy, massage, aura balancing and nutrition.

In spite of all that knowledge and training, it took more than a decade for Madhuri to eliminate a family of inter-related illnesses. She couldn't think, she was irritable and tired and experienced what seemed like premenstrual symptoms every day.

Just as her illness had many facets—including hepatitis, allergies and glandular dysfunction—it required a many-faceted treatment protocol for a cure. She researched and experimented, got help from an MD, a dentist, a chiropractor and a chemist, and through a process of trial and error, she slowly found every key to a cure.

Today, after twenty-six years in the health-care profession, she has a busy natural medicine consultation practice with patients all over the country. When they come to her with little hope left, fearing that they may never be well again, Madhuri understands their despair.

Chapter 9

Tricia Bies

T ricia Bies heard her tumor plop on the floor. There is sat, gray, shiny and quivering, about the size and consistency of an oyster.

She had been undressing to take a shower, and when she leaned over, the breast tumor fell off. She stood looking at it, so shocked she could only stare without speaking. Her chest now had a gaping hole where the tumor had been. "It was like someone took an ice-cream scoop and scooped out flesh," she recalls. She called her husband and a friend. They came to look at the thing. Together they talked excitedly about what had just happened. Deeply religious, they praised God for the event.

Tricia put the tumor in the freezer. She taped a small colander over the bloody hole where the tumor had been. She reasoned that the colander would prevent dirt from getting into the wound while still allowing air to it so that a scab would form. She didn't know what else to do.

She didn't dare go to the doctor; she'd have to admit what she'd done to get rid of the tumor, and she was certain she'd be sent to the mental ward.

Three months earlier, in October 1999, she had noticed a sore spot on her left breast. It felt like a blocked milk duct—something she'd once experienced while nursing. A visit to the doctor for a mammogram and then an ultrasound revealed tumors. "They called it two masses," Tricia recalls.

The news hit her hard, like it had in 1981 when she gave birth to a stillborn baby. "People say they feel they're falling into a deep pit; that's what it feels like. Your mind doesn't want to assimilate it," she says.

The next day, she went in for a biopsy. Three days later, she went back to the doctor for the results. "He said, 'You have infiltrating ductile carcinoma. It's malignant. We can do a radical mastectomy on Wednesday. We want to also take all the lymph nodes under your arm and down your side.'" It was a simple, straightforward announcement. The diagnosis had been made, and so had the treatment decision.

But Tricia didn't want to lose a breast and lymph nodes. She knew that she had options, because her brother had cancer—embryonic cell carcinoma—in 1974. The Mayo Clinic gave him six months to live, but he's still alive today.

So is Tricia.

Chapter 10

Annie Wilkin

Getting to the emergency room would not be easy. Annie lived in the middle of Costa Rica's coffee country, down a dirt road so steep that only four-wheel-drive vehicles could get up it. And she didn't have such a vehicle. She typically took the half-hour hike up the road to catch a bus. But if one of her "episodes" hit, she would not be able to walk.

The episodes began with the feeling of cold liquid running from the back of her head down her spine. Diarrhea and dizziness followed, sometimes with stomach cramps. Then her eyes and throat would swell. It felt as if her body was closing down. The episodes were becoming more frequent, and she wondered what she would do if a severe episode made her unable to breathe.

Her Costa Rican friends had taken her to a doctor in the nearby town of Paraiso. He diagnosed an allergic reaction to ant bites and prescribed medication. But the pills didn't work. She went to another doctor in a larger city. He did blood tests, diagnosed typhoid fever, and prescribed several medications. They didn't help either.

Finally, Annie ended up in a hospital emergency room. The three emergency room physicians talked among themselves in Spanish. They, too, diagnosed allergies but said her reaction was to mosquito bites, not ant bites. They gave her an allergy shot. Annie expected immediate relief, but it seemed as if only time diminished her symptoms. After two hours, she felt well enough to hitchhike home.

Her Costa Rican friends sprayed her house with a pesticide to keep it free of mosquitoes. Later, she learned the pesticide was DDT—an agricultural chemical banned in the United States but still sold to third world

41

countries. Her friends had it on hand, because they used it in the coffee fields all around Annie's house.

Annie's episodes increased in frequency and severity. Finally, she concluded she would have to return to the United States just to stay alive. Certainly, the doctors back home would be better; they would know how to cure her.

But after a year back in the United States, she still hadn't found a doctor who could cure her. Some might provide help and support. But only she could cure herself.

Chapter 11

Jeff Houck

J eff Houck calls himself "a product of modern medicine." He was born three months prematurely in 1952, weighing less than five pounds. In those days, preemies often died. Jeff believes he, too, would have died had his mother not been a nurse at the hospital, which gave him clout with the nurse in charge of his wing. "The charge nurse marched up and down the hall issuing orders that I would be taken care of," Jeff said.

Because he was born before his organs, immune system and respiratory system had fully developed, he experienced numerous illnesses throughout his childhood. He suffered from severe allergies, chronic influenza and pneumonia. By the time he entered college, he was sickly and tired, sleeping twelve hours a day and "living on antihistamines."

After completing two bachelor's degrees in wildlife and fisheries management, he had decided to follow in his mother's footsteps and study nursing. It gave him access to free medical advice from teachers. One of his professors diagnosed Jeff with high blood pressure. "I heard the standard platitude: 'Cut down on salt, and you may have to go on blood pressure medicines the rest of your life.'" But Jeff didn't believe it. "I had more faith in the body," he explains.

Jeff began reading Rodale's *The Complete Book of Vitamins* and *The Complete Book of Minerals for Health*. He created a therapy for himself consisting of lecithin, vitamin B-50 complex, and vitamins A, C and E. "Lo and behold, after awhile, my energy increased," Jeff recalls. "My little black cloud went away, and my blood pressure lowered ten points on average, both systolic and diastolic. I was almost a normal person for the first time in my life."

He never completed his degree in nursing, becoming disillusioned with allopathic medicine. He decided he preferred a naturopathic, holistic approach to healing chronic illness. And so he treated himself with only vitamins and minerals for about fifteen years, "and they did me fine," he says.

Then, in 1993, he began experiencing lower back pain, at times so severe that he would cry out in agony. "I was always able to grit my teeth and get on with life. I told my wife that at least I made it to forty years old before I screamed."

That same year, he suffered his first bout of shingles—painful blisters that erupt when latent viral particles from an old chicken pox infection get reactivated along the nerves. Stress is often cited as the culprit. Jeff had been working in the state prison system for nearly eleven years, and he believes the stress of it nearly destroyed his health. The shingles pain was so severe that he lost his fine motor control and could not, for example, use fingernail clippers.

"If the nerve is inflamed, it's very painful. It's the heaviest, darkest, crippling pain I've ever had, and nothing over the counter will block it," Jeff said. "Kidney stones are awful, but this is worse. It comes on in waves, and all you can do is groan."

The shingles eventually subsided, but a couple years later, Jeff felt pain again, this time in his lower spine. He thought it was due to numerous small injuries over time, such as getting bucked off of horses. He had used chiropractic for minor back pain in the past, and it had always worked well. This time, it wasn't working. He went to a physician who said he may have to consider a spinal fusion. He also tried a new chiropractor. This one took x-rays that showed a healthy spine with no bone spurs and no degeneration of the vertebrae.

"He said my spine looks ten years younger than it is. But I couldn't walk. I was fully incapacitated."

Jeff stayed in bed for the next few days in the same position. At one point, his abdominal and back muscles convulsed, and he felt his vertebrae grinding together. The pain persisted over the ensuing months, and although Jeff could get out of bed, he couldn't do simple tasks such as driving a car. And he still had no idea what was causing the pain.

"I kept looking for anything that would relieve bone pain. I tried vitamins in higher dosages, but it didn't work. I didn't like taking muscle relaxants, because they stop your bowels from moving. I'd stayed away from herbals because of the potential for abuse."

Jeff researched and experimented. And he learned a skill that allowed him to find out what his body needed for healing. Today, he is virtually pain-free.

Chapter 12

Kim Dunn

Kim Dunn's four-year odyssey with illness began one morning in February 1998 when she woke up with flu-like symptoms. She felt tired and weak. The back of her neck ached. She thought it would go away in a day or two. But it didn't. She stayed in bed for the next three weeks, sleeping most of the time, then decided it was time to go to a doctor.

She told the doctor she didn't think she had the flu. "He said, 'Give it a bit more time, and see if it runs its course,'" Kim recalls. But it didn't run its course. So two weeks later, Kim made an appointment with her primary care physician, who ordered a blood test. The results showed she was suffering from the virus thought to cause chronic fatigue syndrome.

Epstein-Barr virus infects up to ninety-five percent of adults in the United States, according to the Centers for Disease Control, but it remains latent until the immune system is so weakened that it can no longer keep the virus in check.

"When I found out it was Epstein-Barr, I was happy to put a face on this enemy. As long as I know what I'm fighting, I can gear up with the right kind of ammunition. I figured that there was a cure," Kim recalls.

The doctor told her the virus could remain active for a year. He told her to get a lot of rest. Kim let it go at that.

But as the weeks turned into months, Kim decided she could not continue to just let it go. She had a persistent, low-grade fever and suffered from insomnia. She caught every cold and flu bug that her children brought home. Her joints began cracking and popping. She was unable to hold her head up for long. She had to stay in bed fifteen to twenty hours a day. And most troubling of all, when she did get out of bed, she often couldn't remember what she'd done five minutes ago.

So she went to the Internet and began researching the virus. "I found out it can turn into chronic fatigue if it lasts more than a year. I was horrified by what I read of people with chronic fatigue. You're a vegetable; you can't function. I would have rather been dead."

Pharmaceutical companies have no silver bullet for viruses. From the view of modern medicine, viruses must simply run their course. "The doctors offered nothing," Kim recalls.

She remembers being frightened, not only for herself but also for her family. She was thirty-six years old, married, and as the mother of two small children, she had a family to help support. "I was depressed and angry and determined to do whatever I had to."

As an attorney for the federal government and a former judge, she was used to tackling projects in a logical, orderly way. So she took what she calls "the portfolio approach" to her illness, researching extensively and devising a six-part plan to bolster her immune system.

The investment of her time and effort paid off. She knew she had begun her recovery when she was free of pain and could get out of bed at eight in the morning.

Chapter 13

Thomas Deer

The doctor called Thomas Deer at seven in the evening. That scared him. "To get a call from a doctor after hours usually means bad news," Tom says. And it was. His kidney cancer had come back; now it was in his lungs. The doctor suggested Tom go to an oncologist, and Tom made the appointment.

He had been diagnosed with renal cell cancer six years earlier and had a kidney removed. The tumors were encapsulated and therefore hadn't spread. That meant Tom didn't need to undergo chemotherapy or radiation treatment. The urologist had been reassuring: Unless a few cancer cells were wandering around in the blood, there was an excellent chance there would be no reoccurrence.

But now it was back. The oncologist explained that renal cell cancer sometimes returns in the lungs, the brain or the bones. A CAT scan showed the largest tumor was next to a main artery in Tom's right lung. The doctors cut into the lung to get a sample of the tumor. The surgeon found the lungs were full of little tumors, and the prognosis was dismal: The average person in his condition could expect to live about ten months.

"I said, 'There's nothing?' He said, 'There are some things we can try, but nothing is very successful.' I said, 'I'd like to talk to someone else.' He sent me to a doctor in Madison. I looked her up on the Internet, and she's famous for dealing with tough kinds of cancer. She gets lots of money for drug trials."

After reviewing Tom's entire collection of CAT scans, biopsies and oncology and radiology reports, the doctor spent an hour discussing Tom's cancer with him and his wife. "I was pretty impressed that she would spend that much time," Tom says. He recalls the doctor saying, "The kind of cancer you have, we aren't very good with. We try Interferon and radiation and new drugs, and sometimes we're able to slow it down or stop it from growing. But we rarely kill it. Once in awhile we do, but we just ask ourselves, wow, how did we do that?" Then she told him, "It seems like you have a good attitude. Go home and live your normal life. If and when you get sick and your quality of life goes downhill to the point you're willing to try something that'll make you even sicker, come back. Meanwhile, you've got a good chance of doing well for awhile."

So Tom took her advice. At age fifty-seven, he retired from his job as a maintenance supervisor at Kimberly-Clarke and planned to relax and spend a lot of time fishing.

"Still, you feel pretty hopeless," Tom said. "You're just waiting for the guillotine to fall."

But Tom decided not to just sit back and wait. More than two years after Tom got his ten-month life sentence, the guillotine still had not fallen.

Chapter 14

Linda Pranzitelli

L inda Pranzitelli didn't want to end up with a colostomy bag attached to her side to catch her feces.

In September of 2000, she had gone to the doctor with stomach pains. A colonoscopy showed that her colon was severely inflamed. The doctor sent her home, saying there was nothing he could do. For the next four months, she had diarrhea. She began losing weight and became weaker, and eventually she was unable to work outside her home.

After four months with no improvement, she called the doctor for more information. "Tell me again what I have and what the prognosis is," she recalls asking. He told her that although she did not yet have Crohn's disease—an inflammatory disease that results in ulceration of the intestines—she would one day. He told her the only thing she could do that might help was to eat a diet high in fiber. He said she would probably have to have a section of her colon cut out in a year or two because it was not returning to a healthy state, and that she could end up with a colostomy bag on her side.

"He offered me no medication or help, he only wanted to eventually get to surgery," Linda recalls. "That's what they all want to do. They cut, the problem goes away, and they get rich and you get sicker."

Linda's doctor had offered the standard allopathic diagnosis and prognosis for her condition. But hearing the standard allopathic solution devastated Linda. She spent the next two weeks crying.

"I wasn't through living. I didn't want to be in a wheelchair with a bag on my side," she said. And so she spent a lot of time praying. She believes the thought that she should get a second opinion was a reply to her prayer.

51

Her second opinion was from a naturopathic doctor who said Linda could do many things in addition to eating a diet high in fiber. As a result, she has been able to avoid the colostomy bag.

Chapter 15

Victoria Boutenko

Victoria Boutenko went to bed every night knowing she might not wake up the next day. Her heart would one day stop without warning. That's what the doctor had said.

Heart disease ran in Victoria's family. Her father had suffered two heart attacks. Her own heart beat erratically, with several slow beats followed by several fast beats. In her home country of Russia, a physician said nothing could be done for the arrhythmia, as it was a genetic condition. The doctor had no advice for curing the condition, only for preparing for sudden death, Victoria recalls. "She said I should have a will written and always wear clean underwear" to avoid embarrassment at the unexpected moment when the ambulance would have to be called.

The doctor recommended Victoria lose weight, so she became a vegetarian, but after four years, it had not helped. The doctor also recommended Victoria take pills, but Victoria refused to ingest the chemical compounds.

Victoria had been a political activist, working to change the Russian Constitution's sixth amendment so that child laborers would be paid for their work. Her activism led to a three-week tour in the United States, which resulted in Denver Community College offering Victoria a teaching job. She and her family decided to stay in the states, because her mother had warned it would not be safe to return to Russia. As immigrants, the family could not immediately afford medical care, so Victoria did not go to a doctor here. In fact, she didn't do anything.

"When I was younger, I was always thinking that if I got sick when I was older, I'd do yoga and jogging. But when I did get sick, I was so depressed, I couldn't think of doing anything serious."

53

In fact, nothing motivated Victoria until the day her son, Sergei, fell into a coma after gorging himself on Halloween candy. The doctors diagnosed juvenile diabetes. They said there is no cure, that little Sergei would have to have insulin shots the rest of his life.

"I was crying all night, sitting in the kitchen asking God why us, why him," Victoria recalls. She felt that having to inject insulin to continue living was the same as being handicapped. And she resolved that Sergei would not live that life. What she had not been willing to do for herself, she would do for Sergei. She would find a cure.

"I had an intuitive feeling the diabetes could be cured, but I didn't know how," she says.

Today, she does know how. Now she has written two books and travels the country teaching what she discovered—a discovery that cured not only Sergei's diabetes, but also her daughter's asthma, her husband's malfunctioning thyroid gland and her own arrhythmia.

BREAKING
THROUGH THE
ILLUSIONS

Die my dear doctor?
That's the last thing I shall do.
—Henry Palmerston,
Prime minister of Great Britain,
1855-1865

Chapter 16

Finding Hope at the End of Your Rope

T he self-healers you've just met hit the end of their ropes and the end of hope. Some were in pain. Some were dying. They were devastated and discouraged. But in the end, they survived their death sentences and recovered from their so-called incurable diseases. Hundreds of thousands of other people with the same diseases have not recovered. So why have the self-healers?

Many factors may have influenced their healings. But two stand out as characteristics they all share: First, they took responsibility for their health. Second, they were willing to look beyond allopathic medicine.

We live in a culture that discourages doing either. We place responsibility for our health on the doctor. And doctors are trained to use only a tiny slice of humankind's accumulated healing knowledge—the slice called allopathy. Allopathy calls our illnesses "chronic" or "incurable" because it does not have the tools to cure them.

And so we slip further down the rope, losing hope that we will ever recover.

Often, it is only when we reach the end of our rope that the first ray of hope appears. One day, there's a chance meeting with an old friend who cured her arthritis or a bit of information on a talk show about a diet for diabetics or a book title that catches our attention. That first ray of hope is often just a fleeting glimpse at the possibility of healing.

Because of our cultural conditioning, we usually don't grasp at the ray of hope. We ignore the advice on the talk show because we'd have to take responsibility for changing our lifestyle. We thank our friend for the

57

information but decide to do only what the doctor recommends. We put down the book.

The self-healers in this book are the ones who didn't.

I want to encourage you to be one who doesn't. When you hear of a possible cure—no matter how far-fetched it seems at the time—don't ignore it just because it's not what the doctor ordered. Follow that ray of hope. It may not be the one that leads to a cure. But at least you'll have done one thing, and that will give you the courage to try one more thing, then one more thing, until something works. You will have said yes to taking responsibility for your health. You will have said yes to accepting healing from any source, not just a doctor.

You're about to find out how the self-healers did this. You've already read about the first part of their journeys, most of which began in a doctor's office. You've seen how they reached the end of their ropes, some becoming depressed or angry, others praying, others preparing themselves to die. Now you'll see how they found their first rays of hope. You'll see how they began to take responsibility for their health and how they began to look beyond the doctor's office to widen their healing options.

In order to do these two things, they had to break through the two illusions: "I'm not responsible for my health," and "I should only do what the doctor says."

This section provides a bevy of facts to begin opening your mind to the possibility that neither of these is true—that each is a myth that keeps us sick. Once you're willing to consider the possibility that these illusions are not true, you can then search for what is. Find your truth. It may lead you back to health.

Chapter 17

*Better health care will depend
not on some new therapeutic standard,
but on the level of willingness
and competence to engage in self-care.
The recovery of this power
depends on the recognition of
our present delusions.*
—*Ivan Illich, Medical Nemesis*

Illusion One:
I'm Not Responsible

Bernie Siegel, MD, author of *Love, Medicine and Miracles*, classified about twenty percent of chronically ill people as survivors. "In other words, they are willing to take responsibility for their condition, redirect their lives and participate in their own recovery," he wrote. About sixty percent want to do nothing but allow doctors to treat them. "The remaining twenty percent are secretly happy to die, because their life is in shambles," he says.[1]

We can understand the first twenty percent and perhaps even the last twenty percent, but what about rest? Why are sixty percent of us content to hand over responsibility for our physical well-being to our doctors?

First, if we take responsibility for getting well, we might have to take responsibility for getting sick. And that's a scary proposition. It means we have to take a brutally honest look at our lives: what we eat, drink and think; how we work, live and play.

Then we have to do something about it. And most people just don't want to. We don't want to change. It's not easy to give up a habit or start a new one. It's hard work. It's so much easier just to let the doctor fix it.

This aspect of human nature is obvious to the doctors who treat us. "Early in my internship, I realized that most of my patients wanted only to be relieved of any symptoms that were causing them difficulty—pain, limping and so forth—so that they could go back to the poor health habits they had before," says Joe Diamond, MD, in his book, *Your Body Doesn't*

59

Lie.

Martha Christy used to fit that mold. She spent years going to doctors, asking them to get rid of the symptoms that were causing suffering. She remained ill for decades, never taking a look at what she might be able to do for herself.

When she finally did take charge of her health, she healed. It was such a transforming experience that she wrote a book about it, *Your Own Perfect Medicine*. The book outlines her healing experience and takes a critical look at the things that keep us sick, including our own lifestyles and habits for which we don't want to be responsible.

She writes, "Every day as a nation, we consumers drink millions of gallons of those toxic brews called Pepsi and Coke; we ingest millions of dollars worth of junk food, food additives and sugar, stuffing it all down at warp speed as we madly propel ourselves through overcrowded streets in cars belching carbon monoxide fumes, all the while breathing in the toxic aroma of the grossly polluted air. Arriving at our synthetically constructed domiciles, we subject our bodies and minds to relentless TV radiation and the dismal harangue of the nightly news, all the while (treating our headaches) with Bayer or Excedrin, Anacin or Dristan, or whatever other wonder drug flashes seductively across the screen. And then we ask ourselves, 'Why don't I feel good—why can't my doctor fix me once and for all?'"

Like Martha, many of the self-healers in this book started their healing journeys with that question: Why can't my doctor fix me? Getting well meant looking at several aspects of their lives—the stress of their jobs, their negative attitudes, the health of their marriages, the chemicals in their homes, the chemicals in their foods, the depth of their spiritual lives. They had to find the courage to look at themselves honestly. Then they had to change those things that might be contributing to their illnesses.

Not one of them says it's an easy thing to do.

"People should know they can have control. But it's hard to take control," says self-healer Tricia Bies. "The weight is on me if I take control. If I don't drink fresh juices, take supplements every day or take enemas, if I don't do that, I'm going to be sick. It's a great responsibility. Most people would rather leave the responsibility with the doctor: 'I'll do what you say, but make me well.'"

To do otherwise could lead to painful emotions. If we participated in making ourselves sick, that's embarrassing. It may make us feel guilty for harming ourselves. But it doesn't have to. We can recognize any feeling of guilt that comes up, then replace it with a plan to get well. The purpose of taking an honest look at why we got sick is not to feel guilty about it, but to see what we can change in order to get well—to recognize what role we can play in healing. If we caused the problem, we can also fix it.

Self-healer Jacquie Compton recalls the guilt she felt after five surgeries left her still dying from cancer. "That feeling of guilt creeps in. You think, maybe it's my fault."

The guilt can either paralyze us into hiding behind the doctor, or it can become a tool for recovery. Jacquie, now a practicing naturopath, often sees patients who feel guilty about their illness. "That guilt thing will make them explore all of their resources," she said. "But sooner or later, what we have to realize is that we are responsible for what goes in our mouth."

In other words, that guilt works best when it's used to increase our options and make us take responsibility.

The Reliance on Professional Opinion

A second reason we're reluctant to take responsibility for our own health is because we rely on specialists for everything. When the toilet breaks, we call the plumber; for pests, the exterminator. We go to the quick-lube shop for a simple oil change, to the beautician or barber to get a haircut, to the doctor for a fever.

Not that there's anything wrong with taking advantage of all these conveniences of modern life. It's just that we've forgotten that in many time periods in may cultures, every person played plumber, exterminator, mechanic, beautician and doctor. There was a time when Dr. Grandma administered most of the family's medical treatment, when Dad fixed all the mechanical breakdowns, when Mom cut everyone's hair. We are capable of learning how to fix our toilets and cars, eliminate pests, cut our hair and cure our bodies. And if doctor after doctor is failing to cure us, we have to remember that we have the ability to gain the knowledge to do it ourselves.

Yes, it takes work. No, it isn't convenient. But if your health is at stake, the effort is worth the cure.

In the movie *Lorenzo's Oil,* based on a true story, little Lorenzo Odone is struck with a rare, genetic disorder that causes his body to dissolve the protective coating surrounding his nerve cells. As the boy slowly loses his ability to see, talk and even breathe on his own, his parents decide to do their own research. They decipher a biochemical riddle that has stumped the experts, and they discover that an extract from simple cooking oils might cure their son.

This is perhaps an extreme example, but it shows that people with no medical or scientific background can find medical solutions to genetic diseases considered incurable by the medical establishment.

The Odones began searching for their own answers when they realized that the medical experts did not have the answers; that if they relied only on professional opinion, their son would die a slow and horrible death.

Many of the self-healers in this book were surprised to discover that the so-called experts did not have the expertise to cure them. It was then that they decided to gain their own expertise.

Consider the story of Michael Romano, an eighty-five-year-old Italian-American who has been drinking a four-herb tea to cure his non-Hodgkins lymphoma and prostate cancer. He's also taking hormone shots recommended by his doctor. But he's not following his doctor's advice blindly. When his cancer indicators dropped to an acceptable range, he decided to wait three months before considering another hormone shot. "The doctor said, 'I think you ought to have a shot.' But it's my body. I might be harming myself, but it's my decision," Romano says.

He translates an old Italian saying: "A mechanic is a mechanic, but the boss is a super mechanic. In other words, the doctor is a doctor, but I'm the super doctor. I'm the last word. Some people will follow the doctor regardless of what he says. Hey, if you feel bad from taking that medicine, quit right then and there. If the medicine is hurting you, stop."

Self-healer Andrew Yachad, born and raised in Africa, noticed that in America, people are "entrenched in relying on professional opinion." He thinks that doctors should encourage patients to take responsibility for their health. But that's a rare occurrence. In fact, many doctors think it's dangerous for the patient to be responsible.

So we're going to have to take the initiative ourselves. Go ahead and get the expert opinion. But also come up with your own opinion based on your own research and reasoning.

Consider what self-healer Kim Dunn did when the doctor told her there was nothing more she could do to rid her body of the Epstein-Barr virus: "I told God, 'I'm going to use the intelligence you gave me to get as far as I can.'" Then she began to use her own intellect to find a cure. She became the expert.

One word of caution: The moment you begin using your own brains to help heal yourself, you might be ridiculed by friends and family.

"Take special note of the fact that if anyone ever gets up off their seats and determines to try something to make them healthier or that will give them a better way of life, people gather around to try to talk you out of it," says Jason Winters, who traveled around the world researching herbal cures for cancer. He faced the ridicule of friends and strangers in his quest, but in the end, he cured himself.

In the third section of this book, we'll take a closer look at facing the disapproval of friends and family when you make your own treatment decisions. Meanwhile, let's look at a third reason why we don't take responsibility for our health.

The View of the Body as a Machine

If your body is simply a jumble of mechanical parts, its breakdowns certainly aren't your fault.

In the mechanical-body model, illness can't possibly be caused by what you eat, breathe or drink. Filling your car with gasoline doesn't cause the car to malfunction. The parts just sometimes wear down, get out of kilter, slip. It's normal, we tell ourselves. Sometimes the problem is caused by a manufacturer defect (genetic disease). Sometimes it's a car wreck (physical trauma). And sometimes it's just everyday wear and tear on the engine (chronic illness). But none of that has anything to do with you. If your body is mechanical like a car, occasional breakdowns are inevitable. They're surely not caused by what you do.

In this view, neither can illness be the fault of what you think and feel. How can your emotions harm a car? How can thoughts damage a machine?

This gives us an easy out. Not only can we give away responsibility for our health, we don't have to be responsible for our unwillingness to be responsible. We trick ourselves into thinking there's a reason why we shouldn't take responsibility for our health. We give ourselves a reason why we should just let the doctor be in charge of our well-being.

The mechanical-body theory still dominates allopathic medicine. It's a four-hundred-year-old theory that was replaced in the twentieth century by the discoveries of the new physics. But "modern" medicine has been slow to catch up.

Scientists now know that the physical universe—and the human body —does not operate like a machine. Cutting-edge science has shown how complex living systems, including human bodies, are much more than the sum of their parts. Quantum physicists have shown that thoughts have an impact on the physical world.

The discoveries of Albert Einstein and other physicists are slowly filtering down to the other sciences. Their concepts are becoming known to the lay public. They're making their way into science books in schools. And one day, they will be the dominant paradigm upon which all the other sciences, including medicine, are based. When that happens, it will be much easier for people to see themselves as responsible for their health.

Before we look at these new scientific discoveries that show why you are responsible for your health, let's look at the old ones that made you not responsible.

For hundreds of years, scientists have dedicated themselves to studying smaller and smaller parts of the physical universe. In medicine, that translates into human bodies filled with organs made of tissues made of cells composed of chemicals made up of molecules.

This is called the "reductionist" view. Combined with the body-machine viewpoint—also called the "mechanistic" view—it led to today's dominant medicine. This is allopathic medicine—a type of medicine that has proven its excellence in fixing broken parts and its uselessness in fixing systemic illnesses such as lupus and MS.

Let's take a quick look at how these reductionist and mechanistic views came to dominate medicine, eliminating your responsibility for your health.

A Brief History of Modern Science

The roots of our conviction that Western medicine is superior are buried deep in the sixteenth and seventeenth centuries, when the Scientific Revolution ushered in a new worldview. It began with Nicolas Copernicus, who discovered that the earth revolves around the sun. Suddenly, the thousand-year "fact" that the earth was the center of the universe had to be abandoned. (Keep this in mind later when we discuss how modern physics is abandoning the four-hundred-year-old "facts" that support allopathic medicine.) Copernicus knew how his theory would upset the scientists of his day, so he waited until 1543—the year he died—to publish his findings, and he presented them as theory rather than fact. (Keep this in mind later when you read how the quantum physicists call their discoveries theories.)

Then along came Galileo Galilei, who came up with a way to prove Copernicus' theory was, indeed, true. He is called the father of modern science, because his method—combining experimentation with mathematics to determine the laws of nature—remains the cornerstone of science today. Galileo told scientists they should not study anything other than the observable properties of things—properties that are objective and can be measured.

Immediately, science—and medicine—became limited. Anything that could not be measured by the day's technology—things such as thoughts, emotions, intuition, the body's subtle energy fields—would no longer be a matter for scientific research.

While Galileo specified what should be studied, Francis Bacon outlined how it should be studied: Come up with a hypothesis based on observations, then create experiments to test it. Immediately, science—and medicine—became limited further. Any medical remedy proven over eons of experience was suddenly discounted as unscientific if it had not yet been the subject of scientific experimentation. Thousands of years of healing wisdom were thrown out the window.

Rene Descartes, the father of modern philosophy, solidified this new viewpoint. He convinced his contemporaries that nothing should be believed unless it could be proven experimentally.

"We reject all knowledge which is merely probable and judge that

65

only those things should be believed which are perfectly known and about which there can be no doubts," he wrote.

Thoughts and emotions already had been eliminated as topics to study in medical research. Now God and faith went out the door.

Descarte's famous statement, "Cognito, ergo sum" ("I think, therefore I am") forevermore separated the mind from the body. It said that man is his mind, and the body simply the mechanical vehicle that carries it. And thus, the mind-body separation began.

When you hear someone speak of the Cartestian worldview, they're talking about Descarte's belief that the only things that are real in the universe are the mechanical parts that can be measured and, when fully understood, controlled.

Previously, the aim of science had been to increase wisdom to allow mankind to live harmoniously based on his understanding of the natural order. Now, science became the tool with which to gain knowledge that allowed scientists to control nature, including the human body. Francis Bacon even suggested nature be made a slave to man.

Isaac Newton, born in 1642, completed the transformation of our view of the universe from a living, organic system to a machine that operates according to unbreakable laws. According to legend, when Newton saw an apple fall from a tree, he had a sudden revelation that the force that pulled the apple toward the earth was the same force that held the planets in orbit around the sun. He had discovered gravity. And he invented calculus to explain the motion of the universe's mechanical parts.

So the view of the universe as a giant clockwork—and the human body as a smaller clockwork—became firmly embedded in the Western mind, among both scientists and the lay public.

And suddenly, people were no longer responsible for getting sick.

If your body is a clock—a mishmash of mechanical parts—they're bound to break now and then. And you're surely not responsible for that. That's what the old—and current—worldview says.

But it's not true. You are much more than a machine. Your body is a whole system of complex, interrelated processes impacted by your thoughts, your emotions, the foods you eat and the environment in which you live. It's not a defective machine with imperfect parts and bad genes.

"We're made in divine perfection, for crying out loud," says self-healer

Sharon Rosa.

So-called modern medicine, however, is stuck in the old Cartesian worldview. "Allopathy schools its patients in the anonymous, invasive, soulless etiology of illness: Illness is disconnected from the individual's life, meaning and direction. It is an inconvenient interruption, an irrational assault, a fixable flaw in the machinery. It has nothing to do with you," writes medical journalist Richard Leviton in his book, *Physician*.

Self-healer Martha Christy agrees, and she puts the responsibility on you, not the doctor, to break out of the Cartesian illusion: "We expect our doctors to behave like mechanics, to diagnose and to fix every possible thing that goes wrong with us, as if our bodies were cars or machines that could be repaired simply by pouring in some synthetic substance or replacing a part. But our bodies aren't machines, and our doctors should be relieved of their role as mechanics that we run to every time we feel sick. Our bodies are immensely intricate, sensitive, individually unique, living mechanisms that need gentle respect and care, not the incessant and routine overkill of concentrated drugs and invasive surgery."

It is this viewpoint that will allow us to take responsibility for our own health, to respect the body's ability to heal itself and our mind's ability to start the process.

The System Perpetuating Itself

We've now lived with the mechanistic, reductionist worldview—and the biomedical model it fosters—for hundreds of years. It's a well-entrenched mindset, so solidified in the Western psyche that it now perpetuates itself.

The depth of the entrenchment can be seen in how much of our power we've handed over. We not only expect doctors to get us well once we're sick, we now expect them to also keep us healthy in the first place.

It's called preventive medicine, and it's a symptom of a system that has disempowered us fully.

Insurance companies now waive the deductible and pay in full for wellness check-ups. The medical community recommends mammograms for women older than forty. We're supposed to be tested every so often to make sure our bodies haven't somehow turned against us. If an imbalance is found, such as high blood pressure or high cholesterol, we are not told how to return the body to its original, perfect balance. Instead, chemical drugs are prescribed. Many have side effects that will later have to be treated by yet another chemical substance. We're sucked into the system. We become perpetual patients.

Preventive care is a relatively new commodity on the market. If you don't take time to stop and analyze it, it will seem benign, even beneficial. But it's a wolf in sheep's clothing, because it further removes your responsibility for your health. It turns health into something you pay for rather than something you achieve. Now, regardless of whether you're well or sick, you're always a patient, always under the doctor's oversight, always powerless to affect your own health. Your only responsibility is to make the appointment and show up at the doctor's office.

But that's not the same as accepting responsibility for your health, just as going to the grocery store is not the same as accepting responsibility for what you eat.

The medical community has given us a proverbial grocery store with few nutritive or chemical-free foods, yet we continue shopping there, content that the food must be all right if the Food and Drug Administration allows it on the shelves.

Pharmacist and author Daniel Mowrey says our trust of the medical system, its chemical drugs and its government backing shows an attitude of reckless abandon toward our health. He says that if the predominant attitude was written down as a creed, it would read: "We shall put our trust in medical specialists to insure we receive adequate nutrition; we shall put our trust in medical specialists to prevent most disease and to cure the rest; and, above all, we shall trust in the government to insure that we aren't poisoned, extorted or misled by those in whom we have entrusted health and life itself... In short, without fear, (we) freely relinquished all individual responsibility for health." (Daniel Mowrey, Ph.D., *The Scientific Validation of Herbal Medicine*, copyright 1986, McGraw-Hill. Material reproduced with permission of The McGraw-Hill Companies.)

With the doctor responsible for both preventing and treating our diseases and the government responsible for making sure it's the best prevention and treatment, we no longer have to consider the health consequences of what goes into our bodies—in the form of food, water and air. We no longer have to worry about how we treat our bodies—in the form of movement, muscle tension and mental tension. We are exonerated. We are not accountable. And we are dying because of it.

Only in North America and parts of Europe have most people thoroughly divested themselves of health responsibility. Most other cultures have retained a viewpoint that has allowed mankind to survive relatively free of chronic disease for tens of thousands of years. They know that full health is the natural state of man—a perfect reflection of nature's perfection—and it is each person's responsibility to retain the balance that maintains the body's health.

The Chinese, for example, believe health is largely a matter of balance, and they consider themselves responsible for maintaining it. If they fail in their endeavor to stay healthy, they consider themselves largely responsible for restoring their health.

Why should we adopt this viewpoint?

Now that we've looked at the reasons why we don't accept responsibility for our health, let's look at why we should. And finally, let's look at how to start.

Reclaiming Your Power

"The single most empowering thing a person can do is to take charge of their own health," says self-healer Jeff Houck.

Every self-healer in this book learned the power of self-responsibility.

"When you have to weigh everything that you put in your system, it's a big responsibility," says self-healer Tricia Bies. "But it also gives you freedom, because I have the freedom to choose what I want to do."

Others see self-responsibility as a moral imperative.

"It's your life, and you need to take responsibility for it. Don't place it in anybody else's hands. You decide," says Arlene Oostdyk, a seventy-five-year-old nurse practitioner whose viewpoint was radically altered by a vision she had in 1957. She had fallen into a coma after hemorrhaging during labor and losing more than half of her blood. Here's how she describes what happened: "I was running down a dark corridor with many doors. After opening several doors and finding figures cloaked in black, I kept running and saw a brilliant light at the end of the corridor. I saw Jesus (but not his face) sitting on a throne with a huge *Lamb's Book of Life* on his lap. There were angels and beautiful music everywhere. He read my birth date and my death date (as November 23, 1957), but said, 'I will add years to her life.'"

That experience, combined with her ensuing run-ins with allopathic medicine, led her to a profession as a licensed nutritionist and herbalist. "I know now it (the coma) was in order to help all these other people," she says. "I feel God has given me a ministry these past twenty years of helping people back to health in all ways: spiritually, mentally and physically."

Oostdyk recommends people take responsibility for their health not only because it's the right thing to do, but because it leads to solutions. It gives you power over your illness. If you take responsibility for your illness, one day you will discover what caused it. And when you know that, you will know what can cure it.

Niro Markoff, diagnosed with AIDS in 1985, is free of the disease today not due to the miracle of modern technology, but due to the miracle of the individual's power over herself.

"I will always be grateful to my doctor for admitting there was nothing he could do, because his honesty forced me to take responsibility for my own life," Markoff wrote in her book, *Why I Survive AIDS*.

But for Markoff, as well as for most self-healers, it isn't an easy thing to do. In fact, most were led to self-responsibility either out of desperation or by chance. If they had only known (as you are learning by reading this) that they didn't have to suffer for months or years until the hour of desperation came along.

Jason Winters reclaimed his power in his hour of desperation. His doctors had diagnosed his neck tumor as infiltrating squamous cell carcinoma. They recommended removing his tongue and jawbone to prolong his life for a few more weeks. He declined the operation and began reading religious books to prepare for dying. Of course he would be drawn to the health references in these books, and he began to notice that every religion talked about the power of herbs to cure disease, including twenty-three mentions in the Bible.

This simple fact changed—and prolonged—Winters' life. Instead of preparing to die, he began researching herbs and preparing to live. He traveled around the world to learn about folk remedies, and he used one to cure himself. Then he wrote a book about it called *In Search of the Perfect Cleanse*. The book quotes a wise Dutch doctor: "Do not be overpowered by sophisticated medical men, for more people die from the mistakes of these men than from their illness... Do not hand yourself to anyone else and expect them to cure you with a pill, for you must heal yourself."

If you don't want to wait until you're weeks away from death, take the Dutch doctor's advice. Make a decision now that you will take responsibility for both your illness and your healing.

One note of caution: You must be prepared to give up the benefits of being sick. You'll have to honestly search your mind and soul to find out whether you're enjoying any aspect of being ill. Perhaps you don't have to face other responsibilities because of your illness. Maybe it gave you an excuse to give up that job you hate. Or perhaps you like the attention you've received since becoming ill. People have fawned over you. You've become the center of your family's attention. Since getting sick, you've experienced an outpouring of sympathy and love. And it feels so good.

If you're not willing to give that up, you won't be able to take charge of your healing.

Once you decide the benefits of being sick aren't worth the cost, the next step is to figure out how you caused your disease.

Exercising Your Responsibility

Motivational psychologists teach the power of a simple exercise in responsibility. They suggest that when someone does something that upsets you, take responsibility for it, even though it seems utterly ridiculous that you're responsible for the other person's words or actions. Ask yourself, "What did I do to create this situation?"

People who practice this exercise a few times begin to see that in most situations, there was something they could have done to prevent the other person's actions. Or they could have responded to those actions in a different way to create a different outcome. By pretending to be responsible, they discover a solution to the problem—something they have the power to control.

So even if you don't really believe it, do the mental exercise of pretending you're responsible for your illness. Ask yourself, "What did I do to create this illness?"

For a minute, stop believing what your doctor tells you. He most likely believes that your disease is caused by a malfunctioning mechanical part, and it malfunctioned because it was genetically predisposed to malfunction, so it's not your fault. If you listen to this, you won't even consider any cures beyond what the doctor offers. And if it's a modern-day disease, such as diabetes or multiple sclerosis, you'll live with it the rest of your life, because allopathic medicine does not know the cures. The doctor believes they cannot be fixed.

If you choose, instead, to take responsibility for your illness, the result will be something other than a dead-end diagnosis.

In the case of multiple sclerosis, instead of having an excuse to do nothing, you will ask yourself, "What did I do to get this?" To answer that, you'll have to start studying MS. If you're like self-healer Annie Wilkin, you'll discover that MS and pesticide poisoning have many of the same symptoms. You'll learn that the occurrence of MS is particularly high in agricultural areas. And you may just decide to try eating chemical-free, organic food while also ridding the body of all the pesticides it already has stored in its tissues. And perhaps, like Annie Wilkin, your "incurable" disease will disappear.

In the case of diabetes, if you take responsibility for it, you may learn that even though you are genetically predisposed to diabetes, it is not a sealed fate. Your research may lead you to discover how diet affects the pancreas. Perhaps you'll discover that emotional stress can damage organs. You may read in a book that exercise impacts insulin production. And through this process, it will begin to dawn on you that your diet, lack of exercise and stress may have caused the genetic predisposition to kick in.

Now you're being responsible. And by being willing to consider what you may have done to cause it, you'll know what you can try to do to cure it. For if diet, stress and lack of exercise caused it, then changing your diet, your stress level and exercise level could cure it. And since you've been doing extensive research, you've probably learned about an herb or two that supports the pancreas in producing insulin.

"The use of basic natural foods and natural medicines, unlike synthetic drugs or surgery, requires a degree of self-love, self-discipline and patience—listening to the body, observing the causes behind the symptoms of our illnesses, and changing unhealthy habits and attitudes, rather than relying on strong medical intervention to mask underlying disease factors by relieving symptoms," says Martha Christy. "No matter how inconvenient these changes might seem now, just wait until you see how inconvenient cancer, heart disease and serious chronic illness can be."

The self-healers in this book learned just how inconvenient chronic and deadly illnesses are. Let's take a look at how some of them came to take responsibility for their health, and how doing so allowed them to find hope.

The more serious the illness, the more important it is for you to fight back, mobilizing all your resources—spiritual, emotional, intellectual, physical.
—*Norman Cousins,*
Anatomy of an Illness

Chapter 18

Self-Healers Take Charge

It was easy for self-healer Kim Dunn to accept responsibility for her healing. She's a high-powered woman who is not intimidated by the mantle of authority our society gives doctors. Her legal career had included a stint as a judge, and she was trained to weigh information calmly and dispassionately and to consider all viewpoints. So when her doctor told her she had the Epstein-Barr virus and nothing more could be done, she didn't accept this standard allopathic opinion as fact. She immediately began doing her own research.

She recalls telling God, "I'm going to use the intellect you gave me to get as far as I can, and the rest is up to you." It was a partnership, not between patient and doctor, but between self-healer and the divine. Her part was to take responsibility and figure out everything she could do to make herself well.

She put together a six-point treatment plan that she calls her "portfolio approach." By eliminating every obstacle to recovery and trying every treatment that might heal her, she acted much like a wise investor who combines numerous stocks into an investment portfolio. Even if some stocks lose value, others are bound to gain. Something is likely to pay off. Several of Kim's "health stocks" did pay off. Because Kim took responsibility for her health, she avoided what could have been a lifetime of suffering from chronic fatigue syndrome.

Self-healer Darla Greenig is one of the few people who never became culturally conditioned to accept the doctor's opinion without question. When she was growing up, her family had a you-don't-get-sick code. So she had almost no experience with doctors. When she finally went to a rheumatologist, he diagnosed fibromyalgia and gave his profession's standard prognosis that nothing could be done beyond taking pain pills. But Darla was not conditioned to blindly believe what the doctor said. That made it easy for her to take responsibility for getting well.

"I thought, I know there's something more I can do, and I'm going to find out." She started by calling her son, who had an acquaintance whose wife had fibromyalgia. This woman had been helped by a clinic in Fort Collins, Colorado. It was Darla's first ray of hope in fifteen years, and she immediately began following it.

Self-healer Jacquie Compton's willingness to take responsibility for her health came from a personality trait that doesn't allow her to give up. She's simply persistent. So when the doctor pronounced Jacquie's death sentence, she began setting her affairs in order. At the same time, she was slowly making the decision not to die.

"I thought, I have to live, because I have to make memories for my kids," Jacquie recalls. "It's that intrinsic factor that sent a message down to the cellular level that I can't die now. And I knew I wasn't going to cave in. I don't like to think of myself as stubborn, but I'm tenacious. I'd been taught that you couldn't quit."

Jacquie began by exploring all the options allopathy had to offer. She didn't know she had any other choices. Then one day, a neighbor suggested she try taking vitamins. "I had no nutritional background at all. I made no connection between what went in my mouth and what my body gave me back. But I listened to her, because I had to make sure I'd explored all my options." The neighbor gave Jacquie some reading materials, and Jacquie decided to research further. She found a book by pioneer nutritionist Adele Davis. Later, in a health food store, she picked up a newspaper and read an article that said Davis had survived bone cancer longer than most other people with the disease. It was Jacquie's ray of hope, and she followed it.

"I decided I had to make some decisions about nutrition," Jacquie said. She also decided she would not consider more operations. "I'm five-foot-one, and I weighed seventy-two pounds when I left the hospital. I had realized there are many more parts they could take out. I had nothing to lose going the natural route."

She had been seeing a doctor, but she stopped. "I became aware that what they were doing was not working, so why am I going there? That's part of intellectual honesty," Jacquie said.

Self-healer Thomas Deer took responsibility for his health slowly, over time. When the doctor said that his lung cancer was incurable and he probably had about ten months to live, Tom simply accepted it. "My wife and I sat down and dealt with death," he said. "We faced it and just decided we'd live life to its fullest until we couldn't anymore." He turned to the Internet, not to search out possible cures, but for support. He found several self-help groups, but he soon gave up on them. "They're so morbid," he said. "They're all talking about dying."

Tom is no longer talking about dying. His ray of hope appeared when a friend mentioned a possible cure. "A guy in my Trout Unlimited group said a relative of his had cancer several years ago, and his wife found this tea, and lo and behold, the cancer went away." So Tom got back on the Internet. This time, he looked up the cancer-fighting tea. "It worked for this guy, so I decided to take it." That decision was an affirmation that he could be responsible for getting rid of his tumors.

At the young age of fourteen, Andrew Yachad was ready to take responsibility for his own healing. In South Africa, like America, relying on the doctor's advice is the conventional thing to do. But Andrew suspected that conventional wisdom is not always so wise. He learned this from his mother, who had eliminated refined sugar and white flour from the family's diet. "At the time, she was flying in the face of conventional society," Andrew said. "I think that gave me the impetus to stand up and say, 'Hey, I'm going to take charge. I won't accept that there's nothing that can be done.'"

So when the doctor told him he'd have to put up with severe asthma the rest of his life, Andrew went to the library. One particular book caught his eye. It was written by a naturopathic physician, Alice Chase, who ran a South African clinic. The diet it outlined gave Andrew a ray of hope, and he's been following it for twenty-five years.

Self-healer Linda Koep had been fully conditioned to put herself in the hands of the medical system. She never considered doing anything other than going to doctors. "You grow up thinking that doctors help you when you're sick. I trusted them completely." But the doctors hadn't helped her. They couldn't figure out the reason for her dizziness, headaches, diarrhea, weight loss, skin rashes and backache. So they sent her to a psychiatrist. The psychiatrist couldn't help her either; his drugs put her in a state of ongoing panic.

Linda's husband was the first to suggest she go to someone other than a medical doctor. So she tried a chiropractor, hoping he could at least relieve her back pain. The chiropractor thought that one of the MD's diagnoses—multiple sclerosis—might be correct. Linda went home from her appointment still without a ray of hope.

One of Linda's former coworkers stopped by Linda's house with a pie and recommended another chiropractor in a nearby town. By now, Linda had nearly given up. After dozens of visits to doctors' offices and hospitals, she did not think one more chiropractor would have the answer. She couldn't afford the luxury of optimism, but she made an appointment anyway.

The chiropractor's office was about twenty miles away. Halfway there, Linda pulled off the road, gripped by despair, and she cried. "I had such a hopeless feeling," she recalls. "But something made me keep going."

The chiropractor talked with Linda for a few minutes. Then he cancelled the rest of his appointments for the day. "He was so interested in my story, and he knew he could help me. It was the first hope I'd felt in months," Linda said.

The chiropractor suggested a treatment team of several alternative health practitioners. They got Linda deeply involved in her healing protocol, and slowly, she began to realize that she could make a difference in her illness. Bit by bit, she took responsibility for her recovery.

Self-healer Annie Wilkin also held the deeply entrenched belief that doctors are responsible for getting us well, so she went only to doctors. If one doctor wasn't good enough to cure her, the only option was to find another doctor. So when three doctors in Costa Rica provided three different diagnoses and prescribed five kinds of pills that didn't work, Annie decided it was Costa Rican doctors, not doctors in general, who were unable to help her.

She had planned to spend years in Costa Rica. But her episodes were increasing in frequency and severity. She concluded that back home, the "better" physicians in the United States would be able to diagnose and treat her.

She wasn't back long before she ended up in the emergency room. She outlined her symptoms to the emergency room physician, happy to finally be able to describe her symptoms in her native tongue. But the doctor, while understanding her words, didn't hear much of what she said. He dismissed all of the symptoms she described except the severe abdominal cramps. He diagnosed gastroenteritis and hinted that the rest was in her head. He sent her home with antacids.

Annie began wondering whether the inability to get a correct diagnosis and find a cure had less to do with the country than with the allopathic medical system. A friend suggested she visit a homeopathist. He was the first of several non-allopathic practitioners who would eventually help Annie recover from an illness that had nothing to do with gastroenteritis. The last practitioner she ever needed was a naturopathic physician who told Annie that she could take responsibility for her own health.

Why did Annie Wilkin have to be told that she could take charge of her recovery? Why did a team of alternative practitioners have to work with Linda Koep before she became deeply involved in her healing? Why did Jacquie Compton have to go through five operations before taking her first step toward healing?

They live in a culture that adheres to two illusions. The first says that people are not responsible for getting sick. The second says that the doctor's medicine is best. It is these two illusions that take away our hope of recovering from chronic or "incurable" illnesses.

Definitions

Allopathic medicine: Treats disease with remedies that produce effects different than those caused by the disease. Also called Western or conventional medicine.

Homeopathic medicine: Treats disease with remedies that cause symptoms similar to those caused by the disease.

Natural medicine: Treats disease by stimulating and supporting the person's natural capacity for healing. Also called complementary, alternative, unconventional or traditional medicine.

He's the best physician
that knows the worthlessness
of the most medicines.
—*Benjamin Franklin*

Chapter 19

Hope Begins
Where Allopathy Ends

L inda Koep, Andrew Yachad, Annie Wilkin, Thomas Deer, Jacquie Compton, Darla Greenig and Kim Dunn all began their healing journeys in the doctor's office. And why wouldn't they? When we Americans get sick, we go to the doctor. It's normal. It's cheap. It's easy. And it's safe. Right?

Well, it's certainly normal in recent decades in North America. Visiting an allopathic MD might be considered abnormal in any other historical era and in most other regions of the world. But during the last blip on the historical timeline (about eighty years) in our little neck of the globe, it's what everyone does.

And it's certainly cheap. Okay, it's the most expensive type of medicine mankind has ever devised, but it doesn't cost *you* much. In fact, after you've paid your insurance deductible, it's free. And if you're really sick, you could end up saving tens of thousands of dollars. Meanwhile, if you went to an iridologist for diagnosis and a reflexologist for treatment, you'd have to pay for it out of your own pocket.

Then there's the convenience. When you get sick, help is just a phone call away. You make the appointment, go to the doctor's office, get a prescription and take the pills. What could be easier? If you don't go to a medical doctor, there's going to be a lot of work involved. You may have to spend endless hours researching your condition. Or you may have to find a competent healer, and that takes a lot more effort than leafing through your insurance company's preferred physician list. The iridologist doesn't advertise in the yellow pages, so you'll have to ask around. And if you want to go to a licensed naturopathic physician, you'll have to travel to one of the twelve states that licenses them. That's so much more effort than popping the top off a plastic orange prescription bottle.

We also go to the doctor because it seems the safe thing to do. The doctor spent at least eight years learning his trade, so he knows a lot more than you'll ever know about the human body. He has all the answers, so seeing him is the only safe thing to do. Right?

Well, not really. Statistics show that allopathic medicine is quite harmful; you'll read them in the next chapter. Yet we've been conditioned to believe it's safe—and not only that it's safe, but that doing anything else is unsafe.

Self-healer Jacquie Compton says we believe allopathic medicine is safe in spite of the statistics because our faith in the medical system has the power of a religion. Doctors are like white-smocked gods who hold our lives in their hands. They can diagnose, prognosticate and prescribe. They can take away your pain or pronounce a death sentence.

"Doctors really are like gods to us," Jacquie says. "Where else can you walk in, and they say, 'Wait for me for two hours,' then they invite you to this inner sanctum and say, 'Take off all your clothes.' Nowhere else do we give people so much power over our time and our body. We've been indoctrinated that this is the way it is. I say it's a religion."

It's usually not until we're chronically ill that we're willing to question the faith. It's only after we learn an illness is fatal that we begin to look beyond what's normal, cheap and easy. People often go through years of suffering before they begin to wonder if the doctor's medicine really is best.

Many self-healers in this book began their healing journeys in the doctor's office. It was the normal and easy thing to do. But it wasn't effective. It didn't work. So they ended their healing journeys outside the allopathic system. To do so, they had to give up the illusion that the doctor's medicine is the best medicine.

A few of the self-healers in this book did not begin their healing journeys in the doctor's office. Some, by the time they got sick, already knew that the doctor's medicine is not necessarily best. Some had broken through the illusion while involved in a family member's healing journey. Others had professional training or other knowledge that allowed them to see through the doctor's-medicine-is-best myth.

Madhuri Cawley, for example, had been a physician's assistant and a pre-med student, and she also had studied several non-allopathic healing systems. When she got sick, she chose the best of both worlds. She went to an MD practicing holistic medicine. He was a doctor knowledgeable about systemic illnesses as well as specific symptoms; about natural medicines as well as synthetic drugs. He had the training to understand the body's mechanics and also to see Madhuri as more than just a bunch of body parts operating in a mechanical fashion.

Jeff Houck also had an allopathic background. He had attended nursing school for a time, and his degree is in biology. "I'm trained as a hard-core scientist," he says. But he also had read up on nutrition, and his scientific training gave him the confidence to try to treat his high blood pressure with dietary supplements, even though it's not what allopaths typically recommend. He put together what he calls a "shotgun therapy" of vitamin C, lecithin, B50 complex and vitamins A and E. It lowered his blood pressure. To his surprise, it also cleared up his allergies. "I understood why these vitamins were working," Jeff said. "They all help the immune system, and allergies are an auto-immune response. They all have some anti-histamine function and help overall body metabolism."

That success with vitamins allowed him to keep an open mind later in life when a more serious condition would require a treatment much less acceptable to modern medicine than mere vitamins.

Tricia Bies had no background in science or medicine, but when her doctor told her he was going to remove her breast, she had a family member's experience to refer to. Her brother's cancer was considered incurable. The doctors gave him six months to live. But the doctors at the clinic in Mexico said he had a chance. They gave him vitamin B17—also known as laetrile. He recovered and has remained healthy and cancer-free for nearly three decades. That gave Tricia the knowledge that she might have an option other than a mastectomy.

Linda Pranzitelli was saved from having part of her colon removed simply because she's an avid reader. Thirty years before showing initial signs of Crohn's disease, she had worked for a woman who used vitamins and minerals and had lent her books on the subject. "I'm an avid reader, and I've been going to health food stores and reading everything since 1978," Linda said.

So when she decided to get a second opinion about her disease, she went to a naturopathic physician who gave her a vitamin B12 shot. "I noticed immediately the difference," Linda said. "I felt grateful, hopeful. Before, I didn't have any hope, and it's pretty hard to live without hope. You have to know what to do to make things better."

For many of the self-healers in this book, hope began where allopathy ended.

So we're going to take a look at just how effective allopathic doctors really are. You'll be in for a surprise. Then we'll look for answers to these questions: If they're so ineffective, why do we trust them? And more importantly, if they're so ineffective, why does the richest, most advanced country in the world have such an ineffective medical system?

Finally, we'll take a look at how the system is beginning to change and become more effective. You'll see how scientific reductionism and capitalism played a big role in making modern American medicine ineffective, and how those very same factors may one day make American medicine work as well as the best healing systems humanity has ever devised.

If you're chronically ill now, you can't wait until the U.S. medical system is fixed. Neither can you afford to hold onto the illusion that the current medical system will fix you. The best way to begin seeing through an illusion is to look at the facts, see the reality. So the rest of this section is a lot of mind-stuff. I hope you'll take the time to read it instead of skipping forward to the heart-stuff—the dramatic stories of the self-healers' journeys back to health.

I hope you'll read both sections, and then decide for yourself whether it's time to dismantle the myth that the doctor's medicine is best.

Who's WHO?

The World Health Organization, founded in 1948 by the United Nations, sets global standards for health and helps countries take advantage of beneficial health technology and information.

Chapter 20

*A truth's initial commotion is directly
proportional to how deeply
the lie was believed.
It wasn't the world being round
that agitated people,
but that the world wasn't flat.
When a well-packaged web of lies
has been sold to the masses
over generations, the truth
will seem utterly preposterous
and its speaker a raving lunatic.*
—*Dresden James*

Illusion Two:
The Doctor's Medicine is Best

L et's say you've decided you're willing to take responsibility
for your health. Now it's time to take action, right? Well, not
quite. First, there's a second illusion that you must thoroughly
dismantle if you want to eliminate the biggest roadblock on the path back
to health. This illusion is deeply ingrained. It's so deeply ingrained in the
American psyche, that it sounds crazy to argue that it's a lie, a myth.

The myth says that the doctor's medicine is the best medicine.

It's not true. Modern American medicine is not as marvelous as most
people imagine.

Just ask some of the MDs who, appalled at the harm caused by their
profession, have dedicated part of their lives to trying to change it—doctors like Stuart Berger, author of *What Your Doctor Didn't Learn in
Medical School*.

Or ask Mary Ruwart, candidate for FDA commissioner in 2002.
Ruwart will tell you that many allopathic medical procedures do not undergo rigorous testing to prove their worth before their introduction. Years
later, when studies are done, the procedures don't always work as expected, she says. She should know. She left her position as an assistant
professor of surgery at St. Louis University Medical School in 1976 and
spent the next twenty years in medical research, developing drugs for The

Upjohn Co. In her book, *Healing Our World: The Other Piece of the Puzzle*, she explains how alternative therapies have been excluded from our system of medicine.

If you need more than professional opinion, look at the official statistics. For example, a report by the government's Office of Technology Assessment says that less than twenty-five percent of all drugs and medical procedures prescribed by MDs have been demonstrated in controlled clinical trials to be useful. That means that if you go to a doctor, more than three-quarters of the procedures in his arsenal have not been proven to work. That's not opinion. It's fact. It's not myth. It's truth.

Yet we have the illusion that the doctor only uses treatments that have been tested and proven in very scientific, objective, double-blind studies. We believe this because many doctors criticize their competitors' therapies as unproven. Goldenseal root to fight an infection? Unproven. Kinesiology to diagnose? Quackery! So say the doctors when they're quoted in the press. But they fail to hold their own methods to the same standard. Allopathic treatment after treatment fails to be proven effective in double-blind studies, yet your doctor still uses them to treat you.

Meanwhile, competitors' treatments that have been proven through rigorously controlled, double-blind, independently researched experiments are automatically dismissed as bunk. MDs are trained to assume no scientific proof is available for medicines and procedures that are not endorsed by the American Medical Association. They automatically tell you there's no proof regardless of whether they've researched it.

Consider chelation therapy—an alternative method of treating heart disease by draining toxins and metabolic wastes from the body while increasing blood flow. Most MDs don't offer it for fear of losing their licenses. They will therefore tell you that chelation therapy has not been proven effective. Yet it has.

When researchers L. Terry Chappell, MD, and John P. Stahl, PhD, reviewed nineteen objective studies evaluating the effectiveness of so-called EDTA chelation therapy, they discovered it works very well. The studies were done on a total of nearly 23,000 patients. The researchers discovered that eighty-seven percent had registered clinical improvement. In one study, fifty-eight of sixty-five bypass surgery candidates and twenty-four of twenty-seven people scheduled for limb amputation were able to cancel their surgeries. Their findings are reported in the book, *Questions from the Heart*.

If the efficacy of this treatment—which is much safer and much less expensive than bypass surgery—has been proven in more than a dozen scientific studies, why won't your doctor use it?

The next few chapters will answer that question, and in doing so, they will chip away at the strong illusion that the doctor's medicine is best.

A Mere Hiccup on the Continuum

The History of Medicine:
2000 BC - Here, eat this root.
1000 AD - That root is heathen, here, say this prayer.
1850 AD - That prayer is superstition, here, drink this potion.
1950 AD - That potion is snake oil, here, swallow this pill.
2000 AD - That pill is artificial, here, eat this root.
—Author unknown

Medicine has been practiced in one form or another throughout human history. That means hundreds of cultures around the globe—from the smallest tribe in Guatemala to the greatest civilizations—have created healing practices over tens of thousands of years. Modern allopathic medicine's two-hundred-year history is a mere hiccup on the continuum. It represents a miniscule fraction of humankind's accumulated medical knowledge.

If you're sick and can't get well, or if you have a disease that could kill you, why would you eliminate more than ninety-nine percent of the world's medical arsenal from your treatment protocol?

According to the World Health Organization, between sixty-five and eighty percent of all people on Earth rely on non-allopathic medicine for their primary health care.

WHO has not fallen prey to the myth that the allopathic doctor's medicine is best. It has broken through the illusion, because it knows the facts. For example, in 1993, it ranked the United States eighteenth among industrialized nations for its level of good health. It said healthier nations allow alternative modalities to openly compete in the medical marketplace. In contrast, the United States has a medical monopoly enforced by state laws and federal agencies.

WHO believes allopathic medicine is not best. It has chosen traditional Chinese medicine as the system that should be propagated worldwide to meet the health-care needs of our time.

China's traditional medicine shares three concepts with medical systems around the world that have endured for millennia. They all are based on the premises that:

- A state of balance is necessary to maintain health.
- Nature has a tendency to heal itself.
- Mind and body are interdependent.

In most other civilizations in all other eras, medical men worked to enhance what occurs in nature. If wounds naturally heal, what would help them heal faster? If natural immunity overcomes bacteria and viruses, how can this natural ability be enhanced?

Even the so-called father of modern medicine, Hippocrates, recognized that all living organisms have inherent healing forces. He called them "nature's healing power" and said the physician's job was to create favorable conditions for these natural forces to do their healing work.

Hippocratic medical philosophy shares much in common with most of the healing systems practiced throughout history in all parts of the world.

"Through the ages, healing has been practiced by folk healers who are guided by traditional wisdom that sees illness as a disorder of the whole person, involving not only the patient's body but his mind, his self-image, his dependence on the physical and social environment as well as his relation to the cosmos and the deities. These healers, who still treat a majority of patients throughout the world, follow many different approaches, which are holistic to different degrees, and they use a wide variety of therapeutic techniques. What they have in common is that they never restrict themselves to purely physical phenomena, as the (allopathic) model does," says physicist Fritjof Capra in *The Turning Point*.

These other healing systems, with their herbal concoctions and low technology, are just as effective as allopathic medicine and more widespread. They are not chicanery, as American doctors would have you believe.

Practitioners of other systems of medicine not only have many more centuries of experience to rely upon, they also share the qualifications of allopathic doctors: They are part of a professional elite practicing medicine based on a written tradition.

The practitioners of these systems of medicine might be amused if they heard an allopathic MD criticize their work as unscientific. They might wonder at his hubris. What kind of distorted and illusory thinking would make a person discount thousands of years of empirical knowledge? It's allopathic medicine in the Western world that has limited experience and only a tiny accumulation of knowledge.

Allopathic medicine is so young and so inexperienced that it hasn't had time to be truly tested and proven. Without the accumulated knowledge of centuries, its patients are little more than test subjects—human guinea pigs whose lives will show whether allopathy, in the long run, proves effective.

Does two hundred years of severely limited medical research in America have more credence than tens of thousands of years of direct experience elsewhere?

Our medical system, by saying yes, has limited the number of options available to heal you to a tiny fraction of what has healed others. The vast majority of available cures—including those that are the most widely used worldwide—are not offered by physicians in the United States, because they are labeled alternative.

"We can't say that alternative therapy is really alternative. After all, the so-called alternative therapy has been around since the beginning of man. It's medicine and drug companies which are relatively new so are in effect the alternatives," writes Jason Winters.

After Winters got "incurable" cancer, he began searching for answers and turned first to the Bible and other religious texts. "It doesn't mention anything about cutting, chemotherapy and radiation in the Bible. Buddha never spoke of it; neither did Jesus. Maybe they thought it wasn't worth speaking about," he wrote.

Winters then traveled the world looking for cancer cures. In his travels, he discovered remedies that are nearly universal because they've been proven to work—not by a double-blind experiment financed by a drug company, but by millions of people who have used them over the centuries.

For example, he found that more than thirty countries have the same remedy for congested kidneys: Squeeze a lemon into a glass of warm water each day and drink it.

Like many self-healers, the knowledge Winters gained by doing his own research made him question why the allopathic medical establishment keeps Westerners away from so many cures proven effective through anecdotal evidence.

"The North American Indians did not spend billions of dollars each year on research to know that chaparral is a great blood purifier. It certainly is and they use it daily," he wrote. "The Russian lumberjacks did not spend millions on research and pay scientists high salaries to tell them that if they rubbed DMSO on their swollen hands, the pain and the arthritis would go. They still use it every day. The gypsies of Europe did not spend billions to find out red clover is a great medicine and blood purifier. By consuming it, they recover from illnesses, including asthma and lung problems, and feel great."

Self-healer Martha Christy came to the same conclusion after suffering for years, then finding a natural cure that her doctors never told her about.

"At this point in time, we need to stop examining and picking apart therapies that have hundreds, and in some cases, thousands of years of practical experience behind them," she wrote. "Rather than wasting their time and our money on the unnecessary contortions of trying to 'scientifically' prove what hundreds of thousands of patients have already experienced over many centuries with these simple and safe natural techniques, the National Institutes of Health and their panel of experts' efforts would be infinitely better spent on deciding how to formulate new and inexpensive FDA guidelines for approving traditional medical therapies and in qualifying responsible health care practitioners for both conventional and natural medication."

Until that happens, the doctor's medicine will not be the best medicine. In fact, it might be the worst.

The medical establishment
has become a major threat to health.
—*Ivan Illich*

Chapter 21

First Do No Harm

The first principle of the Hippocratic Oath, to which every doctor must swear, is "Primum, non nocere," which translates, "First, do no harm." And yet allopathic medicine is killing us in greater numbers than it's curing us.

We have a system that not only fails to cure us but often harms us. And many of the treatments that harm us weren't necessary in the first place. To shed further light through the illusion that the doctor's medicine is the best medicine, let's look at each of these elements and the facts that contradict the myth.

The American Medical Association (AMA) estimates as much as one-third of all illness may be iatrogenic (caused by medical therapies), according to *The Informed Consumer's Pharmacy*. The book reports that only ten percent of people who visit doctors would benefit from drugs or surgery, yet nearly two-thirds come away with prescriptions.

In 1998, the Institute of Medicine released a report saying medical mistakes in hospitals kill up to ninety-eight thousand Americans a year. Two years later, the *Journal of the American Medical Association* tried to lessen the blow. It published a study saying the previous studies were flawed because the doctors hadn't agreed on what constitutes a deadly error. Nonetheless, the institute didn't back down on its concerns.

Unlike the AMA—an organization protecting the financial interests of an industry—the Institute of Medicine has nothing to lose or gain by admitting the facts. It is an organization chartered by Congress to advise the government on scientific matters. In March 2001, it recommended an urgent overhaul of the medical system, saying too many Americans get inadequate or unsafe therapy. Modern American medicine damages patients too often and routinely fails to help them, the institute report says.

Many doctors are alarmed by the harmfulness of the procedures they must use. Some have written books to alert people to the dangers they face—MDs like Stuart Berger, whose illusions about allopathy were shattered while he was in medical school. His mother had been diagnosed with cancer and recommended for chemotherapy. Berger suggested she get a second opinion. The second doctor did exploratory surgery and discovered that the "mass" that the other doctor wanted to treat with toxic chemotherapy was a simple, benign cyst. "She had come only days away from being pumped full of the most lethal, debilitating agents—drugs quite capable of crippling or even killing her—for a cancer she never had... Her life could have been forfeited to delay, mismanagement, the needless toxic interventions of a medical system run amok," Berger wrote.

From then on, he saw through the myth that most of us believe—the myth that doctors offer their patients the best medicine.

"I recall one day in medical school, shortly after I began making rounds on the wards, having a sinking revelation that hospitals, just like any other human enterprise, are just a vast interlocking constellation of human foibles, frailties and failings. People screw up, confusion abounds, politics fester, neglect occurs, greed persists. Things are, in short, no different than in a corporation, a neighborhood, or a Girl Scout troop. The stakes are just higher," Berger wrote. "Deadly drugs, dangerous diagnostics, rampant infections, slipshod procedures—clearly, the best thing you can do for your health is to stay as far away from hospitals as possible," he added.

After finishing his residency, Berger continued to pay attention to the facts that shatter the doctor's-medicine-is-best illusion. All he had to do was read report after report in his professional journals about the amount of damage done by doctors. One report said twenty-five thousand people died as a result of *needless* surgery one year. Another showed that out of one hundred patients who had developed serious kidney problems while in the hospital, more than half had problems caused by hospital procedures and treatments, including x-ray dyes, blood supply and antibiotics.

Berger concludes, "The secret is out that our nation's way of healing is sick indeed."

But is the secret really out? How many doctors are really concerned about the state of their profession? And how many patients really know how dangerous allopathic medicine is?

The self-healers in this book are some of the patients who do know.

"People are being killed by their therapies," says self-healer Darla Greenig. She recalls a conversation she once had with a friend with cancer, Tricia Bies, another self-healer you've met in this book. Bies was explaining that her oncologist wanted to give her chemotherapy. "He said, 'We have drugs to take care of the nausea, drugs for swelling, other drugs to take care of the sores in the mouth, and you should also eat white flour and white rice for diarrhea.' She said, 'Can you think of a faster way to get rid of me?'"

Here's an oncologist, prescribing and advising according to his profession's highest standards, yet it's obvious to the patient that this cure is worse than the disease.

Self-healer Arlene Oostdyk, a registered nurse, doesn't pull any verbal punches in assessing the frailties of allopathic medicine. She says the damage it causes is so obvious, that only idiots wouldn't see it. "They radiate cancer patients, then they tell us radiation causes cancer. Do they think we're some kind of dummies?"

She points out that allopathic practices are now the third leading cause of death in America—a fact reported in several of the allopathic profession's own trade journals.

The proof has been around for a long time. When social critic Ivan Illich turned his social research skills to the study of the modern medical system in the 1970s, he concluded that the practice of allopathic medicine poses one of the gravest dangers to human life and health, and he called modern medicine "one of the most rapidly spreading epidemics of our time."[1]

Like Berger, Illich was alarmed by statistics showing that dangerous medical techniques that aren't even necessary often cause additional damage. For example, he discovered that more than ninety percent of all tonsillectomies performed in the United States are unnecessary, yet about one quarter of all children still underwent the operation. They not only experience the stress of an operation, but in addition, parts of the body that enhance immunity—the tonsils—are removed, potentially compromising the children's future health.

Illich also discovered that doctors often don't have accurate information from which to diagnose. For example, he found that up to one-quarter of simple hospital tests show seriously divergent results when done from the same sample in two different labs.

Robert Schneider is another medical doctor alarmed by his profession's standard practices. In his book, *When to Say No to Surgery*, he estimates that up to eighty percent of all surgeries are unnecessary, and more than eighty thousand patients die each year from surgeries they didn't need in the first place.

Deadly Drugs

If you think unnecessary surgeries, faulty procedures and bad lab tests are a problem, look at the statistics on pharmaceuticals.

- Between 100,000 and 150,000 Americans die each year from FDA-approved pharmaceuticals used as directed.[2]
- Drug mistakes—made either by the doctor or the patient—kill an additional 140,000 patients a year in the United States.[3]
- Medical drugs kill more Americans every year than car wrecks.[4]

"I firmly believe that if most of the pharmacopoeia were sunk to the bottom of the sea, it would be all the better for mankind and all the worse for the fishes," said Oliver Wendell Holmes.

Chemical drugs are toxic agents, rarely the best medicine, yet we rely on them without question. About two-thirds of all visits to a physician end with the doctor filling out a prescription, according to Gideon Bosker, MD, author of *Pills That Work, Pills That Don't*.

Sidney M. Wolfe is another doctor concerned about this deadly epidemic of prescription medication. In his book, *Pills That Don't Work*, he writes, "You go to the doctor because you don't feel well. You are listened to (sometimes), examined, tested and then the doctor usually writes one or more prescriptions for you. You go to the drug store to have the prescriptions filled. You go home and start taking the pills. Now everything will be all right, right? Wrong. Neither you nor, in some instances, even your doctor realizes that one out of every eight prescriptions filled... is for a drug not considered effective by the government's own standards. Since all drugs involve risks, this lack of effectiveness means you are exposing yourself to dangers without gaining compensating benefits. In other words... these drugs are not safe."

The statistics are even worse for over-the-counter drugs that do not require prescriptions. Wolfe helped write another book titled, *Over The Counter Pills That Don't Work*. He became concerned after serving on one of the FDA's over-the-counter-drug advisory panels, which are made up of physicians, pharmacists and scientists. These panels reviewed about 300,000 drugs and found that only about one-third of the drug ingredients were shown to be safe and effective for their intended uses. The FDA's director of over-the-counter drug evaluation, Dr. William Gilbertson, reported that FDA officials did not implement the findings of its panels, because they were pressured by drug companies not to.

Now you can start to see who has a stake in keeping you hoodwinked by the illusion that the doctor's medicine is best.

The Incurables

Another way to see through the illusion that the doctor's medicine is best is to simply look at the high percentage of people with chronic and incurable illnesses in nations where allopathic medicine dominates.

Approximately 100 million Americans are considered chronically ill. Why can't our medical system cure the diseases suffered by nearly a third of our population?

The true irony of allopathic medicine is that it not only causes more damage, it also fails to heal the original complaint.

Imagine any other profession trying to survive under these circumstances. Imagine an accountant who not only was unable to complete your tax return, but the work he did accomplish resulted in you getting penalized by the Internal Revenue Service. Or imagine an attorney who not only failed to win your lawsuit, but the work he did resulted in you getting sued.

We might be willing to put up with the liver damage caused by the asthma medication or the bronchial damage caused by the liver medication if it would just cure what it's supposed to cure. But most chemical medicines aren't designed to cure; they're designed only to mask symptoms. You take aspirin for your headache. Are the pills designed to eliminate the muscle stress that caused the headache or only to take away the symptom? You take insulin for diabetes. Is it meant to restore your pancreas to proper function or only to eliminate the symptom?

Allopathic medicine is perhaps the only health-care system in history that is not focused on healing—on eliminating the cause of the illness. And perhaps that is why one in every three Americans has an illness that allopathic medicine cannot cure—for that is all that a chronic illness is—a disease that allopathic doctors don't know how to cure. Consider that the so-called incurable illnesses—diabetes, some cancers, hypoglycemia, multiple sclerosis, heart disease, asthma, arthritis, lupus—are not considered incurable in many other cultures.

Phantom Diseases

Allopathic medicine, with its high-tech gadgetry and life-saving speed, is highly effective at emergency and trauma care. Crush your arm, and there's no better medical system to save it. Suffer a heart attack, and all that gadgetry can keep you alive. But contract a simple virus, and there's nothing the doctor can do to get rid of it. There is still no cure for the common cold—at least not at the doctor's office. And if you get a serious illness, like AIDS or hepatitis, you're really out of luck if you live in America. You will not be offered a cure.

You'll be in even worse shape if you suffer from an illness that doesn't fit neatly into the physician's diagnostic manual. The symptoms suffered by many Americans are difficult to quantify and classify. They leave medical doctors mystified and impotent. And they often leave patients labeled hypochondriacs.

Dr. Berger calls them phantom diseases and says, "Because of the vague, systemic, sporadic symptoms they can often produce—particularly in their early or borderline cases—they form a whole class that is often overlooked in the slam-bam high-tech-diagnostic way we do medicine... But that doesn't mean such diseases aren't very real—and that they don't cause tremendous human suffering."

These diseases include systemic candida, chronic fatigue, hypoglycemia, food sensitivities and hypothyroidism. They're systemic illnesses—something many allopathic physicians aren't trained to work with. They're trained in the one-agent-one-cure method of medicine, leaving them powerless against these conditions, which become chronic without proper treatment.

The resulting tragedy, says Berger, is that "patients—particularly women—may find themselves branded as 'hypochondriac,' manifesting 'hysterical symptoms.' Perhaps this is... simply a way of saying, 'I can't find anything,' and so taking the physician off the hook. I can't enumerate how many patients recount tales of being ignored, patronized and pooh-poohed when they try to explain their vague problems."

You'll recall Linda Koep, who ended up at the psychiatrist's office because her back felt dizzy—a symptom that several physicians did not know how to categorize. Taking psychiatric drugs nearly made her insane. She almost became a perpetual patient, imprisoned by a medical system that does not know how to diagnose systemic illnesses and has no idea how to cure chronic ones.

Chapter 22

Some experts say that the real true way
to excellent health is so easy
that people can't accept it.
If it doesn't involve drugs and
mutilation, loss of savings
and terribly difficult terms,
then it just could not work.
—*Jason Winters*

Roots of an Illusion

If research on iatrogenic disease and statistics about bad test results, harmful drugs and patient dissatisfaction all show that the doctor's medicine may not be the best medicine, why do we solidly believe it is?

Two of the reasons are simple: We're impressed by high tech and hoodwinked by fancy words.

Doctors certainly give the impression that they know what's best for us. They're so learned that we can't even understand what they're saying when they talk to us about our illnesses. But medicalese does not necessarily mean our doctors are knowledgeable about healing; in fact, it can show lack of knowledge.

Berger complains of his profession's "too-frequent ignorance and inability to give our patients much more than a fancy name for what ails them."

He goes on to say, "It is no accident that we have enshrined such ignorance into our medical lexicon. If you need proof, you only have to look at the whole basket of fancy, Latinate terms we have coined to mask our shortcomings. We have 'essential,' as in essential hypertension, which means that the condition is just there and we don't know why. 'Idiopathic' is another such term, meaning 'without known cause,' as is 'cryptogenic.'...a whole dictionary of diagnoses simply boil down to names for things we don't understand."

If your doctor does not know what ails you, would you prefer he tell

101

you or that he hide behind his techno-jargon?

One of the reasons holistic practitioners are helping so many chronically ill people is because they're not trained to label everything before beginning their healing work. They see the body as a system of innumerable interwoven subsystems connected to a mind and a spirit that impact them all. They don't expect to be able to pinpoint a problem immediately. And they don't need to disguise their initial bafflement with fancy words, because they know that complicated systems can't be easily shoved into a box with a label. So they're not embarrassed to tell a patient, "I don't know why you're sick." Even before assigning a label, they can begin giving the body what it needs to heal.

By contrast, Berger calls his colleagues' know-it-all approach "macho medicine." And part of macho medicine is all the sophisticated electronic equipment that sees into us, through us, classifies and categorizes every part down to its elemental makeup. Put simply, we're bedazzled by high-tech gadgetry.

The procedures are spectacular, too. The surgeon pries open the rib cage, takes a vein from the leg and sews it onto the heart. How can we fail to be impressed? We tend to stop questioning whether less invasive treatments are more effective or why the doctors didn't teach us how to avoid clogged heart arteries in the first place.

The technical jargon, impressive procedures and modern machinery help build the illusion that allopathic medicine provides the most advanced, effective health care on the planet. And, if you live in the United States, it's the only thing readily available. How disheartening to think it may not work very well. How can you have confidence that you'll get well unless you stick to the myth?

These are some of the roots of the illusion. Now, let's take a look at its deepest root.

Ending the Scourges

In the late 1800s and early 1900s, diseases such as typhoid, tuberculosis and cholera still plagued modern man. Now we are nearly free from these scourges. We've been told it's due to allopathic advances, such as immunization and antibiotics. From this root belief, our faith in modern medicine grew.

But is it true?

"Studies of the history of disease patterns have shown conclusively that the contribution of medical intervention to the decline of the infectious diseases has been much smaller than is generally believed," says physicist Capra.

He goes on to summarize the work of public health specialist Thomas McKeown, who took an in-depth look at the history of infections and found that doctors did not play the main role in lowering the death rate from infectious diseases. The end of the scourges came about mainly due to better nutrition, better hygiene, improved sanitation and lower birth rates.

Modern medicine claims the credit, but its magic bullets—antibiotics and immunizations—were not developed until after the major infectious diseases had all peaked and declined. For example, about ninety percent of the decline in childhood deaths from measles, scarlet fever, diphtheria and whooping cough occurred before the introduction of antibiotics and widespread immunization, according to the Bulletin of the World Health Organization.

"The conclusion to be drawn from these studies of the relation between medicine and health seems to be that biomedical interventions, although extremely helpful in individual emergencies, have very little effect on the health of entire populations," Capra says. "The health of human beings is predominantly determined not by medical intervention but by their behavior, their food, and the nature of their environment. Since these variables differ from culture to culture, each culture has its own characteristic illnesses, and as food, behavior and environmental situations gradually change, so do the patterns of disease. Thus the acute infectious diseases that plagued Europe and North America in the 19th century, and that are still the major killers in the Third World today, have been replaced in the industrialized countries by illnesses no longer associated with poverty and deficient living conditions but, on the contrary, with affluence and technological complexity. These are the chronic and degenerative diseases—heart disease, cancer, diabetes—that have aptly been called 'diseases of civilization,' since they are closely related to the stressful attitudes, rich diet, drug abuse, sedentary living and environmental pollution characteristic of modern life."

Allopathy did not end the old epidemics, and it's not having much luck with the new ones, either.

A Brief History of American Medicine

Late 1700s: Midwives attended much more than births. They treated the sick and injured with herbal teas, salves and purgatives. For difficult conditions, doctors were called in to do surgery or bloodletting and give the patient drugs—most commonly opium mixed with digitalis. Doctors were typically judges or merchants who did doctoring on the side.

Early 1800s: Academic medicine edged out the midwives as men expanded their medical practices to full-time professions.

Mid 1800s: The Popular Health Movement returned medicine to its original roots in herbal remedies and support of the body's natural healing ability.

Early 1900s: Many competing ideas and methods were available to the sick, including allopathic, homeopathic and "drugless" systems. Medical boards and licensing exams allowed practitioners to practice any of the healing methods.

Mid 1900s: Pharmaceutical industry influence on medical societies, licensing boards and medical schools had effectively limited American medicine to allopathic drugs and surgery.

Late 1900s: Consumers turned in large numbers to non-allopathic medicines and methods, and the allopathic monopoly reacted by beginning to co-opt some of the more popular "complementary and alternative" methods.

*Unless we put medical freedom
into the Constitution,
the time will come when medicine
will organize itself into
an undercover dictatorship.*
—Benjamin Rush, MD,
signer of the
Declaration of Independence

Chapter 23

How a Medical System Gets Sick

So the allopath's magic bullets are more mythical than magical. All the facts—about cure rates, doctor-caused illness and patient satisfaction levels—contradict the illusion that the doctor's medicine is the best medicine.

How could this be? Is it possible that the most advanced, powerful nation in the world is clinging to an ineffective—even harmful—medical system?

It's not only possible, it was inevitable. Due to a confluence of social, political and scientific factors at just the right time, allopathic medicine gained a foothold, and then a stranglehold, on American health care.

It has been able to do so due to four hundred years of scientific reductionism, the rise of capitalism, the human tendency toward competition and aggression, the cultural value of external power and a host of other influences.

So it doesn't do any good blaming the doctors.

"The average doctor believes strongly in what he's doing, but he's bound into a system that's telling him, only our way is right. And certainly the insurance system has it that way. The doctor's hands are tied from trying anything outside what the AMA approves," says self-healer Jeff Houck, whose background includes experience in both allopathic and energy medicine.

Physician and author Stuart Berger also blames the system rather than the people who work in it. "The truth is that we are all at risk simply because of how our medical system functions," he says.

Edward Bach, a physician who discovered the healing power of homeopathic flower preparations, began expressing concern about the medical system in the early 1900s when it began its rise to prominence. Bach's fellow doctors labeled Bach's treatment method quackery. But he reserved his criticism for the system, not the physicians within it: "It is the system which is mainly wrong, not the men; for it is a system whereby the physician, from economic reasons alone, has not the time for administering quiet, peaceful treatment or the opportunity for the necessary meditation and thought which should be the heritage of those who devote their lives to attendance on the sick."

Medical journalist Leviton points out that even the system has some merit; its intention is to heal people, but it limits the offering of healing options. "In all fairness, it must be said that the medical establishment does want to rescue us, reimbursable patients as we might be, but strictly on its terms," he writes.

And physicist Capra explains why it's important to see that the medical system is simply an outgrowth of larger cultural influences: "During this phase of revaluation and cultural rebirth, it will be... crucial to go beyond attacking particular social groups or institutions, and to show how their attitudes and behavior reflect a value system that underlies our whole culture and that has now become outdated."

Social critic Illich views the medical monopoly as a symptom of an industrialized society in which people are simply cogs in a world focused on producing products for maximum profit. Health-care in such societies is designed to repair the human parts of the production machine, he says.

So, instead of angrily accusing physicians of creating a medical system that doesn't work very well, we have to look at the social underpinnings of the system in which they are caught. We'll take an in-depth look at how capitalism and scientific reductionism became the pathogens that sickened the system. But first, let's take a quick look at a few other things that play a role.

The first very human trait shared by doctors is the belief in the correctness of our beliefs. Add duality, and you add the contra-indication of a belief: If what I believe is true, then anything other than that belief must be false. Berger calls this "medical myopia," but it's certainly a trait common to the thinking of most humans in the Western world.

Berger also laments the inability of physicians to keep up with new medical findings. How can any doctor keep abreast when the information is so pervasive that it takes sixteen thousand medical journals published worldwide to contain it all? "With biomedical knowledge currently doubling every eight years, the gap between a doctor's knowledge and the state of the art is a chasm that no doctor can fully bridge," he says.

So doctors can't keep up on their own system of medicine, and they won't consider any other system.

Berger also examines cultural biases that impact the practice of medicine. He points to a classic study in which a researcher at Dartmouth Medical School determined that a woman is eighty percent more likely to have a hysterectomy if she lives in the South.

"One can't help but suspect that such figures reflect more about attitudes held by southern male physicians about their female patients than about any biological reality," Berger says.

He also points to statistics showing that the hightest levels of hospital injuries occur in July, when new medical trainees begin their rounds unsupervised.

"Clearly, in a medical establishment that practices diagnosis by zip code and treatment by calendar, something is very wrong—and very dangerous," Berger concludes.

When Berger opened his own practice in an exclusive area of New York, he saw what he called "veterans of the medical mill"—smart, motivated patients who had "puzzled doctors, ineffective treatments, and mountains of medical bills." The medical system, Berger says, is letting them down. "They don't need a medical quick fix, but a way to take control of their own health and well-being. Yet, at every turn, they find themselves running up against a system that denies them the help they need to stay well, reinforces them for getting sick, and whose powerful tools often make their conditions worse instead of better. These people don't need wonder drugs, crash programs or the crazy prescriptions of the latest health fads. What they do need is a way to break the sickness cycle, see through the hype and the obfuscation, and learn how to get and keep themselves as healthy as possible... They are—and I have no kinder term for it—victims of our institutionalized medical ignorance."

Berger concludes: "One could not have designed a more efficient system to keep America unhealthy."

Now, let's look at the factors that came together to help create this allopathic system of medicine.

Chapter 24

The more we study the social problems of our time, the more we realize that the mechanistic world view and the value system associated with it have generated technologies, institutions, and lifestyles that are profoundly unhealthy. Many of these health hazards are further aggravated by the fact that our health-care system is unable to deal with them appropriately because of its adherence to the same paradigm that is perpetuating the causes of ill health.
—Fritjof Capra

Mechanistic Medicine

Let's look first at how scientific reductionism, which grew out of the mechanistic worldview, created a medical system that's unable to cure chronic and degenerative conditions.

Earlier in this section, we looked at how the mechanistic worldview arose during the sixteenth and seventeenth centuries. We also saw how it made us give up responsibility for our health. (If your body is simply a jumble of mechanical parts that occasionally breaks down, how can you be responsible for that?) And we saw how the mechanistic viewpoint leads to reductionism, or the study of smaller and smaller parts. (The body has organs made of tissues made of cells made of molecules.)

With these backdrops, medicine was bound to come up with the germ theory of disease—a theory that blinds medicine to the causes of complex, systemic illnesses, and that keeps it from discovering the cures.

The germ theory says that specific microbes cause specific diseases. This theory came about when reductionist thinkers, looking for smaller and smaller parts, created microbiology. They discovered that people with a cold had a virus in their bodies. They saw that infected wounds were filled with bacteria. These microbes, they concluded, must cause the cold

111

and the infection.

This is what you were taught in high school biology, and this is what most allopathic physicians still believe.

Non-allopathic healers, on the other hand, take a holistic and systemic approach. They know the body hosts a multitude of bacteria. Seeing the body's ability to keep them in check, they conclude that when microbes flourish to the point of causing disease, it's due to a breakdown in the system or some sort of imbalance. Their goal is to get the body back in balance, help the many interacting parts function well again, so that the body may do what it was designed to do.

For example, candida albicans is a naturally occurring fungus in the intestinal tract, important to digestion. Stress, antibiotics, pesticides in foods, toxic metals in fillings, ingestion of too much sugar, or some combination of these factors can cause an overgrowth of the fungus, leading to a disease called candidiasis. The body was not attacked from the outside by a disease-causing microbe. It was put into a state of imbalance by its owner or by its owner's doctor prescribing antibiotics, which kill the bacteria that keep candida in check.

The candida microbe is beneficial when the system is healthy and balanced. It becomes pathogenic only when the system is weakened or imbalanced.

Most medical doctors still have a difficult time dealing with candidiasis. Some claim it does not exist. They simply don't have the intellectual framework to understand how it works. It doesn't fit with the one-agent, one-disease theory.

"The doctrine of specific etiology has influenced the development of medicine enormously... by shifting the focus of biomedical research from the host and the environment to the study of microorganisms," says Capra. "The resulting narrow view of illness represents a serious flaw of modern medicine which is now becoming increasingly apparent."

Microbes, Capra explains, are not what cause the damage that disease does: "There seem to be very few infectious diseases in which the bacteria cause actual direct damage to the cells or tissues of the host organism. There are some, but in most cases the damage is caused by an overreaction of the organism, a kind of panic in which a number of powerful, unrelated defense mechanisms are all turned on at once. Infectious diseases, then, arise most of the time from a lack of coordination within the organism, rather than from injury caused by invading bacteria."

Disease is not an attack from outside; it's a breakdown from inside. Medical problems cannot usually be reduced simply to one microbial phenomenon. That is a simplistic explanation—a symptom of an immature science that has not grown beyond reductionism.

And so our medical system does not heal us. It occasionally relieves symptoms, and it can fix broken bones and torn tissues. But it does not have the sophistication necessary to heal the systemic problems that cause chronic conditions such as asthma, heart disease, allergies, multiple sclerosis, arthritis, cancer and lupus.

A Side Note

In the next several chapters, you will learn how powerful men manipulated American medicine for personal gain. It may seem a harsh critique. But remember, they simply mirror the society from which they emerge. It is up to all of us to change our society to one based on compassion and concern for the greater good. Only then will we no longer suffer from the greed of a few people with money and power.

*Health care is being converted
from a social service to
an economic commodity,
sold in the marketplace
and distributed on the basis
of who can afford to pay for it.*
**—Dr. Arnold Relman, former editor,
New England Journal of Medicine**

Chapter 25

Monopoly Medicine

America's economic system is capitalism. The system is based on this assumption: If people are allowed to pursue their self-interest by producing and selling goods in a self-regulating marketplace, it will result in the well-being of society, because businesses will be forced by competition to use their resources in ways that satisfy consumers.

This assumption is generally correct. But when people pursuing their self-interest find ways to eliminate competition, capitalism no longer serves society. Recognizing this, we passed anti-trust laws in the early 1900s to stop corporations from creating monopolies.

But somehow, we missed what was happening in medicine. In the health-care business, there were no large corporations buying out all similar businesses of smaller size. There was no medical Microsoft trying to manipulate markets. So we did not recognize what was happening. Doctors didn't try to eliminate the competition from each other. Instead, they joined together to eliminate the competition from non-MDs. It was associations, not corporations, forming a monopoly. And we were not prepared to deal with—or even recognize—the threat posed by thousands of individuals joining together to monopolize a particular service.

And so the doctors, with the help of drug companies, formed a monopoly right under our noses.

In the nineteenth century, homeopaths and herbalists had the largest share of the medical market. They did not try to control the market; their treatments simply worked better. That never changed. What did change was political control of the market.

115

At the beginning of the twentieth century, the American Medical Association commissioned a national survey of medical schools. Newly formed foundations—including those set up by drug company investors, such as the Rockefellers—had huge sums of money to give, and the AMA wanted those funds channeled into certain medical education institutions. The AMA's survey, published as the Flexner Report in 1910, set up strict guidelines for the teaching and practice of medicine. Those guidelines allowed allopathic education and practice only, and they are still followed today.

With this decisive victory, the AMA began to systematically eliminate its competition. Today, it is the nation's largest trade group for medical practitioners; nearly half of American doctors belong to it.

It has close ties with the major trade group for drug companies, the Pharmaceutical Manufacturers Association. And together, the AMA and PMA hold sway over the government agency charged with keeping consumers safe from bad medicine: the U.S. Food and Drug Administration.

Together, the AMA, PMA and FDA form a monolithic medical complex that has completely monopolized medicine in the United States for half a century. Their system of medicine is highly technological, effective for acute care, ineffective for chronic care, aggressive, invasive and very profitable for doctors and drug companies.

"The human body's blood is red, but the lifeblood of our medical system is most decidedly of another hue: green," says physician and author Stuart Berger, who laments how the profit motive can outweigh the healing motive. He refers to a Northwestern University study of patients who had been "dumped" by Chicago for-profit hospitals at a public hospital. Of these, eighty-one percent had no job. The researchers said they were transferred mostly for economic reasons, and that these dumped patients died more than twice as often as other patients.

"One can't help wondering how many of those people would be alive today if hospitals looked more at the medical chart and less at the ledger book," Berger says. He adds, "It's not that medical capitalism cannot coexist with medical compassion, but right now, there is a real question whether they do."

After seeing firsthand how the medical monopoly would rather protect its financial interests than find a cure for her son, Michaela Odone, who is portrayed in the movie *Lorenzo's Oil*, told *The New York Times* that doctors and patients do not share the same interests.

The doctor's interests may include helping his profession hold onto the biggest share of U.S. medical expenditures—a huge sum that continues to grow. In 1940, medical spending accounted for four percent of the nation's gross national product. By the mid-1990s, it had more than tripled to fourteen percent, and it keeps growing. Americans now spend more than one trillion dollars a year on health care. That's about three thousand dollars per person. And the doctors and drug companies get the lion's share—not by producing superior products and services, but by controlling the market.

How do they do this? It took nearly a century to achieve. During that time, the monopoly slowly built four strong legs underneath itself:

1. A controlled medical education system.
2. Restrictive licensing laws.
3. Controlled medical research.
4. A restrictive insurance reimbursement system.

Add the FDA's efforts to squelch information about alternative medicine, and the result is a monopoly capable of curtailing unprofitable treatments and preventing real healers from practicing their healing arts.

"The political issue is the control of the American medical marketplace... and the suppression of true freedom of choice by the consumer," medical journalist Leviton says.

Let's look at each of the four legs on which the monopoly stands and how this stable structure has been able to curtail cures that it does not control.

*Fifty percent of what we have
taught you is wrong.
Our problem is that we don't know
which fifty percent.*
—*Dr. David Greer, Dean of Medicine
at Brown University, quoting
a fellow educator in a speech
to a graduating class*

Chapter 26

The Academic Peephole

The late Dr. Roy Barnes was a gifted healer who could eliminate your pain, increase your energy level and improve your overall health in one half-hour appointment. He practiced chiropractic, learned several ancillary systems of diagnosis and healing, and developed some of his own original techniques as well. But he was unable to find an audience in the United States interested in learning his techniques. His methods were too far outside of mainstream concepts for American practitioners—both physicians and chiropractors—to accept. In China, however, the medical profession welcomed his training visits and asked him to return again and again.

The techniques worked. In one country, they were accepted and adopted by medical practitioners. In another country, they weren't.

Dr. Barnes explained why American practitioners were unwilling to try his techniques. "Most people's peepholes are only this big," he used to say, curling his fingers to form a circle, then putting the circle up to his eye and looking through it. It's simply human nature to look at only a small fraction of what's out there, he explained.

And that's what has happened in American medical schools. The classes they offer cover only a small portion of the available diagnosis and treatment techniques. They focus on allopathy and block out ninety-nine percent of the rest of medical reality. Certainly the students learn that other treatment methods and philosophies of health exist, but they're told that these techniques have little or no value, that the only methods worth studying

119

are allopathic. The medical school peephole is very small, indeed.

Perhaps it has to be, due to the sheer volume of information contained within allopathy. Dr. Greer said that when he used the quote at the beginning of this chapter, it was in the context of rapid advances in medical knowledge. So overwhelming is the volume and pace of new information in medicine that physicians and medical students can't keep abreast of it all, let alone learn about recent developments in non-allopathic health sciences.

In nursing school, self-healer Jeff Houck learned to consider only drugs and surgery as solutions to medical problems. He said he believes that holistic treatments are cut out of the curriculum because they don't generate large profits. "It all leads to the student in the colleges being taught, 'Only our way is right,'" he said.

When Berger was a medical student, his mother almost died due to what he calls "the excesses of medicine gone mad." As a result, he began examining what he wasn't learning that he should be learning. "I recall looking over at my classmates during one grand rounds and worrying, Are we just learning to accept a whole system of medically approved blind spots?... We were learning immense amounts, but were we learning what we should? We were becoming doctors, to be sure, but were we becoming better healers?"

He continued to analyze his training against the measuring bar of how much it would truly help patients. Here's what he discovered: "The system believed it was important that we know how to drive a sharp, hollow needle into a person's living chest without anesthetic in ten seconds in an emergency room, but never taught us how to help our patients live so that they would never be brought into that emergency room. We learned how to use scalpels, deadly drugs and radiation beams to destroy cancer, but not how the right food and lifestyles could help prevent cancer in the first place."

Berger laments not only the narrow range of health care that medical students learn, but also that they graduate not really knowing what's going to be effective for their patients.

Worst of all, Berger says, they don't tell their patients that they don't know.

*One wonders how many people
have suffered needlessly over
the past 75 years
because licensing laws have
suppressed alternative therapies.*
**—Mary Ruwart,
candidate for FDA commissioner**

Chapter 27

The Licensing Lockout

A llopaths gained control of medical schools. Then they built the next leg of their monopoly by the device of licensing laws.

Licensing of doctors had been tried in the United States in the early 1800s, but it was abandoned half a century later precisely because it created a monopoly for the predominant medical practices, which at the time included bloodletting and use of leeches. The physicians of that time concluded that licensing laws were preventing competent healers from helping patients. They also saw that the laws were hindering both innovative research and effective alternative therapies. So they eliminated licensing laws.

But in the 1920s, allopathic organizations again opted to use the device of licensing laws, and they began lobbying state governments to pass medical practices acts. Soon, all fifty states had laws making it illegal for anyone other than a physician licensed by a board of other MDs to diagnose medical conditions and treat patients.

The purpose was to set up a medical monopoly. And it worked. By 1938, students of homeopathic, osteopathic and chiropractic medical schools could no longer qualify for licensing as medical doctors.

Ruwart says that leaders within the AMA knew that limiting who could practice medicine would lead to higher incomes for those allowed to practice.

"Evidence suggests that the pass-fail rate of qualifying examinations

121

may even be adjusted by the licensing boards to keep numbers of service providers (including physicians) low," Ruwart says. "Choice is diminished, and fees rise accordingly."

They certainly did. In fact, the price of medical care soared following the passage of licensing laws.

The public is told that it's worth it, because it makes medicine safer. But is that argument valid?

Sue Blevins, a medical analyst for the Cato Institute in Washington, D.C., determined that it is not. Very little evidence exists to support the contention that licensing laws protect patients or ensure a higher quality of care, Blevins wrote in a policy analysis. Instead, she said, it creates a medical monopoly enforced by the government, preventing competition and making health care costs exorbitant.

The fact that medical licensing laws are designed to create a medical monopoly was confirmed by the courts in 1987 when they found the AMA guilty of breaking anti-trust laws by using the political power of licensing laws to try to destroy the chiropractic profession.

Licensing laws do not truly protect the public from people who would sell us useless treatments. They just keep us from buying treatments— both useless and useful—from anyone outside the monopoly. This leads to the silly situation of a remedy being declared useless one day and beneficial the next. It's useless while in the hands of non-allopathic companies, and suddenly becomes useful when the monopoly controls it.

"Through the licensing process, certain types of unproven procedures (e.g., surgery) are permitted, while others are arbitrarily banned as quackery," says Ruwart, who used to teach surgery at a medical school. "Such unscientific selection has often led to the comical situation of yesterday's quackery becoming tomorrow's cure," she writes. As an example, Ruwart refers to an article in the 1982 *Congressional Report on Quackery* that states there is no remedy for baldness. She then cites Upjohn's introduction of Rogaine™ in 1986; the company hailed it as a prescription medication "proven effective for male pattern baldness."

By the device of licensing laws, certain health products and practices are kept from the public until the power elite is prepared to profit from them. The number of patient options and the quality of patient care are both diminished. The cost of care is put out of reach for lowerincomeAmericans. And the illusion that the doctor's medicine is best is solidified.

"Spellbound by the mystique that surrounds the medical profession, our society has conferred on physicians the exclusive right to determine what constitutes illness, who is ill and who is well and what should be done to the sick," says Capra. "Numerous other healers, such as homeopaths, chiropractors and herbalists, whose therapeutic techniques are based on different, but equally coherent, conceptual models, have been legally excluded from the mainstream of health care."

The more money meddles in medicine,
the more it muddles medicine.
—Stuart Berger, MD

Chapter 28

The Risk of Healing

T he third leg on which the medical monopoly stands is the insurance industry—both the part of the industry that provides medical coverage to patients, and the part of the industry that provides malpractice insurance to doctors. They work together to ensure that both patients and doctors use allopathic medicine. And they turn health care into a commodity to be bought and sold in the medical marketplace.

Stuart Berger recalls attending a symposium at which he was asked to select the most significant medical development of recent decades. He didn't choose genome mapping or CAT scanning. He chose a single sheet of paper: the insurance form.

"Actually, it isn't the paper itself that is significant but the immense for-profit bureaucracy that lurks behind it. Together, they have transformed the face of American health more than any other tool, drug or procedure," he says. "No longer is healing a private matter among doctor, patient and family. Today, some of the most powerful players in the health-care system are those concerned not with health but with money. Theirs is a bottom-line approach to health. Ensuring accessible, high-quality care is not their main goal; generating dividends is. That should make all of us more than a bit concerned."

Insurance companies, by limiting what types of treatments they will pay for, limit the treatment options made available to you as a patient.

"Only those treatments for which they reimburse will flourish and be accepted; those they don't support are consigned to medical oblivion. That has meant that our most innovative, prevention-oriented, common-sense approaches...are not covered," Berger says.

It's accountants, not doctors, deciding how to heal the sick. And they're reinforcing the illusion that the doctor's medicine is best by paying only for allopathic treatments.

If medical insurance locks out alternative treatment, malpractice insurance throws away the key. You can't sue a doctor for malpractice as long as he used the recommended procedures and drugs. And allopathic procedures and drugs are the only ones recommended. Physicians can be found liable only if they failed to perform the standard allopathic treatments. The problem is that the standard treatments inflict damage. Those treatments are administered by well-trained and well-meaning men and women who accept the prevailing standards of their profession even though they see what harm is being done.

This leads to an unusual situation: Doctors using conventional medicine are killing and injuring thousands of patients every month, and by law, they cannot be punished. Meanwhile, physicians using unconventional medicine are healing their patients, but this is illegal, and when caught, they are punished, regardless of how many people they cured.

Self-healer Sharon Rosa remembers what happened when she went into a coma and a hospital physician used an unconventional treatment to revive her. "My doctor lost the right to practice for a few weeks, because he saved my life. They took away his license because they thought he was whackadoo. They didn't understand why he was thinning my blood. They said that's not what the protocol calls for."

Sharon was so transformed by her healing experience that she became a naturopathic doctor. Her state's licensing laws prevent her patients from filing insurance claims to pay for her treatments. They have to pay out of pocket, and that limits both their medical options and Sharon's income.

While Sharon has seen how medical insurance limits patient options, self-healer Jacquie Compton has seen how malpractice insurance does the same.

Jacquie, who also became a naturopath after healing from chronic illness, recalls a time when she gave a cousin herbs for cancer. When the cousin reported to her oncologist that she was taking herbs and felt much better, the doctor dropped her as a patient. "He said, 'You have to get a different oncologist, because I won't treat you, because you're taking herbs,'" Compton recalls. "He said it invalidates his malpractice insurance, and if she dies, he can be held liable."

Insurance company control over health care has three results: It maintains allopathy's monopoly on medicine. It leads to unnecessary procedures as doctors try to protect themselves from lawsuits. And the cost of medicine soars.

The Public Citizens Health Research Group estimates that Americans spend more than ten billion dollars a year on unnecessary surgeries. Why? Consider the old saying well known among doctors: "When in doubt, cut it out." That way, if the patient sues, the malpractice carrier will cover it.

"When it comes to surgery, the free-market principles of supply and demand create a paradox: There are simply too many people in whose interest it is to subject other people to surgery," Berger says.

It's no wonder that our costs for medical care are skyrocketing. While the cost of living increases a few points a year, the size of medical insurance cost increases are in the double digits. Premiums for employer-sponsored plans rose eleven percent in 2001, growing to 2,650 dollars per person, according to a study by the Henry J. Kaiser Family Foundation. As a result, nearly half of all companies are considering taking some of the increase out of employees' paychecks, the study said.

And so the insurance industry continues to bring in billions of dollars while forcing us to use useless medicines and causing us to undergo unnecessary operations, all the while bolstering the illusion that the doctor's medicine is best.

Chapter 29

*If people let government decide
what foods they eat and what medicines
they take, their bodies will soon
be in as sorry a state as are the souls
of those who live under tyranny.*
—Thomas Jefferson

Of Mice and Medicines

The nation's largest drug company makes its money off the harm that doctors do. Amgen sells only five drugs. Its annual sales in 2000 were 3.2 billion dollars. Four of its five drugs do not treat any natural illness. They treat the side effects of other allopathic treatments.

Allopathic medicine makes drug companies rich. Natural medicine makes them poor.

The pharmaceutical industry makes money by supporting allopathic treatments, including its own pills, which make and keep you ill. In other words, what's harmful to you is good for drug companies. In 2000, they spent nearly sixteen billion dollars on advertising campaigns and other marketing ploys that perpetuate the illusion that the doctor's medicine is best.

Your doctor is simply a pawn on the chessboard of these giant corporations. And these mega-firms are simply working to do what all businesses in a capitalistic society try to do: increase profits.

The drug industry makes no money if you find out about cures for heart disease and other chronic ills. It doesn't sell the natural remedies that cure these diseases, because they can't be patented.

"There is an entire industry with an innate economic interest to obstruct, suppress and discredit any information about the eradication of disease," says Matthias Rath, a German physician who came to the United States in 1990 to become the first director of cardiovascular research at the Linus Pauling Institute.

It wasn't always this way. Let's look at a bit of history to see how the pharmaceutical industry evolved as the strongest leg of the medical monopoly.

The Pure Food and Drug Act, passed in 1931, established the U.S. Food and Drug Administration. Its purpose was to ensure Americans consumed safe food and pharmaceuticals.

Before that, Americans decided for themselves what drugs to take. They heard anecdotal evidence from friends who had used various treatments or asked the advice of their pharmacists or physicians. They read *Ladies' Home Journal* and *Collier's* magazines to find out about new drugs and to get new information about side effects discovered for old drugs. These magazines published the findings of groups such as Consumers' Research, which tested pharmaceuticals in laboratories that were independently funded.

The drug companies, too, did advance testing. "Most manufacturers realized that killing the customer was bad for business and did safety testing before marketing their drugs," Ruwart says. The AMA had a Seal of Approval Program that helped consumers make their drug choices.

Then government got into the act. State governments began passing physician licensing laws. The federal government empowered the FDA. Suddenly, Americans' medical treatment options were limited to physicians approved by the AMA and chemical substances approved by the FDA. Unlike the consumer research groups that did independent studies in the past, the FDA would simply review the testing done by drug companies.

And so the drug companies, with the help of the AMA and the FDA, closed the monopolistic fist into a tight grip. Health care in America would no longer be based on the best medicines but on the biggest moneymakers.

Follow the Money

"In our century, drug companies, and the medical researchers they hired, took the job of making and experimenting with medicines away from doctors and the public and withdrew into their laboratories," writes self-healer Martha Christy. "Simple, inexpensive medicines like herbs, homeopathic remedies or urine therapy that have been shown to be just as effective, safer and much less expensive than chemical drug compounds may be better for the public, but they're no good for drug company profits and are therefore not promoted and sold."

Consider the economics of antibiotics. Their over-use is creating so-called "super bugs" that have developed resistance to antibiotics. These strong strains of bacteria are more deadly than their ancestors of earlier generations. So drug companies race to patent new antibiotics for the super bugs. They can expect to make 200 million dollars a year for a drug targeted to treat a small range of bacteria and as much as one billion dollars annually for a broad-spectrum antibiotic. Antibiotics alone add nearly three billion dollars a year to drug company coffers.

Convinced by the drug industry's marketing machine that antibiotics are a modern miracle, patients insist on prescriptions. If a doctor has any qualms about being little more than a salesman for the pharmaceutical firm, he can justify promoting a certain antibiotic by reading about its safety and effectiveness in his medical journals.

But just how reliable are these journals? Most receive about half their income from drug company advertising. That alone should cast suspicion on the credibility of their content. But much worse is the fact that the studies showing a drug's safety and effectiveness are most often funded by the very companies that will benefit from their sale.

To promote Valium™, for example, Hoffman-LaRoche spent 200 million dollars over a ten-year period, paying two hundred doctors a year to write articles for scientific journals. It gives new meaning to the term "controlled studies."

In addition to controlling and paying for the research, drug companies pay for and provide all the information for the Physician's Desk Reference, which is the most widely used reference text on drugs. More than three-quarters of all doctors consult it regularly to find out drug uses, side effects and recommended dosages. Included in its pages are three thousand toxic drugs.

A survey of physicians who have written treatment guidelines for common chronic ailments found that more than half received research funding from drug companies, and thirty-eight percent had served as drug company employees or consultants. Fifty-nine percent had ties to pharmaceutical companies whose drugs were considered in the drafting of the guidelines they wrote. These survey results were reported in the January 30,

2002, issue of the *Journal of the American Medical Association.*

So doctors do not learn about new drugs from independent and objective scientists but from the drug sellers. Pharmaceutical firms not only provide much of the information doctors use to choose a treatment, they also provide incentive for doctors to prescribe their products. Physicians qualify for prizes such as trips and household appliances if they "sell" specified amounts of certain drugs.

The U.S. drug industry spends nearly twice as much a year on advertising and promotion as it spends on research and development, according to a 2001 Associated Press story.

All of this leads to a medical system that is focused on delivering pills —pills that are sold in spite of being unsafe and ineffective—and the suppression of alternatives to chemical pills.

With the doctor's-medicine-is-best myth bolstered by the monopoly, any medicine that's not a profit maker gets put under the rubric "alternative" and dismissed. These are usually natural substances that are less expensive and do no harm, but they're not studied in the drug industries' research labs, because they can't be patented. Therefore, evidence of their efficacy remains mostly anecdotal.

"I'm trained as a hard-core scientist, and I say they're cutting out more than half of their ability to do experiments because they don't grant funding for studies of things that have worked anecdotally," says self-healer Jeff Houck.

When the government, rather than the drug companies, funds the research, it is still limited to allopathic substances. FDA commissioner candidate Mary Ruwart explains why: "Research proposals are evaluated by committees composed of established scientists and physicians. Having served on such committees, I have seen why innovative ideas that do not fit mainstream thinking never get funded. Each evaluator gives the proposal a score; even a single low rating is enough to prevent funding."

She points out that even Linus Pauling, who won a Nobel Prize for chemistry, had difficulty getting federal funding to research vitamin C as a cancer treatment.

On the rare occasion that natural, safe substances do get research funding, that research somehow shows that the natural, safe substance doesn't work. Interestingly, that's the conclusion only of research conducted in the United States, where the pharmaceutical industry holds its tightest grip. The same research done elsewhere often shows that the natural substance works.

You're more likely to get objective test results in Germany, for example, where one in three substances prescribed is an herb.

The geographic bias against non-drugs is shown by research into the efficacy of vitamin B17, or laetrile. It was tested in more than two dozen countries. Researchers outside the United States concluded it was a valuable cancer fighter. But in the United States, the first laetrile study accepted by the medical system concluded that laetrile is useless for cancer. Why the difference in research results? Self-healer Jason Winters points out that laetrile got a passing grade in all the countries with socialized medicine, which means that "they are interested in anything that will prevent illness or heal it inexpensively" rather than in those things that will enrich drug companies.

Self-healer Tricia Bies doesn't care what the researchers say. The anecdotal evidence (i.e., vitamin B17 cured her brother's cancer) was enough to convince her to eventually leave the United States so that she could try it for her own cancer. Had she lived in a country with a medical system not based on biggest profits, she may have been offered vitamin B17 right away, eliminating much suffering.

"There are far more people making a living from cancer than dying from it. If the riddle were to be solved by a simple vitamin, this gigantic commercial and political industry could be wiped out overnight," says G. Edward Griffin in *World Without Cancer.* The book explains how corporations colluded to get laetrile outlawed in spite of the evidence that it cured cancer.[1]

Finding the Healing Fountain

"In this age of high-tech drugs,
plastic body parts and mechanized medicine,
I sincerely hope that all of us
can become more open and accepting
of this natural way of healing the body."
—Martha Christy

Martha Christy came home from the hospital weighing eighty-nine pounds. Her hope had dropped more than her weight, because the gynecologist told her she might be facing a lifetime of corrective surgery.

"Given the state of my health at the time, I couldn't envision that 'lifetime' meant anything more for me than a few additional years of mind-numbing pain and misery before my body final gave out," Martha wrote in a book about her ordeal. "It seemed that death would have been a blessing, especially so that my family could be freed from the seemingly never-ending burden of my illness and be able to get on with their lives."

Martha had borne that burden since her teens. Between ages eighteen and thirty, she had been diagnosed with numerous illnesses, including pelvic inflammatory disease, a thyroid disorder, ulcerative colitis and mononuclesis.

"Any visit to a doctor's office only resulted in another discouraging failure," she recalled. "I felt like a ping-pong ball, bouncing from one drug to another as my doctors kept prescribing more and different drugs to counteract the side effects of the ones I was already taking."

So she turned to natural health, trying vitamin therapy, acupuncture, chiropractic treatment, a nutritional regimen and numerous herbs, and she began to slowly get better.

But when a difficult pregnancy threw her into to tailspin, she returned to allopathic medicine for a solution. Doctors found and removed endometrial tumors, then they removed her uterus. But the tumors returned.

After five surgeries in five years, she lost faith in the doctors and decided to again turn to alternative treatment. She went to a clinic in Mexico for mega-vitamin and live-cell therapy.

"I watched as many of the cancer patients around me seemed to get better and better with treatments. And I did, too—for about two months."

Then Martha started feeling worse again, and the natural therapies that previously had seemed to be working no longer did. By the time she had another bleeding tumor removed in a sixth surgery, she had lost hope that she would ever be able to enjoy life.

Then came the synchronistic event—an event that seems to be a hallmark of the healing process for anyone who has refused to simply hand over her health to the doctors. This synchronistic event is usually a chance meeting or a bit of information that comes along when the last ray of hope is nearly extinguished, when you just don't have the energy or the heart to try anything else.

For Martha, it happened when her husband met a woman who had cured herself of a so-called incurable disorder using a free, natural substance.

Martha wasn't interested. It seemed as if she had already tried most everything that allopathic and natural medicine had to offer. It would be just one more disappointment. But her husband didn't give up. He researched this natural therapy and brought information to Martha to read. She decided to give it a try.

"This simple, natural method may seem less glamorous than commercial drugs and space-age surgical techniques, because it's not glorified by the press or hyped by sophisticated, sugar-coated advertising themes. But when all the man-made medicines in the world can't help, people like myself have been eternally grateful to find that nature has provided this safe, painless solution to even seemingly incurable illnesses." That's what Martha writes in her book, *Your Own Perfect Medicine*. Then she reveals the cure.

Urine. That's it. Martha drank her own urine. And she healed.

She also researched. She discovered that urine, although commonly viewed as a dirty byproduct of digestion, is actually a sanitary, nutrient-loaded substance similar to blood, and that when these excess nutrients are reintroduced into the body, "they boost the body's immune defenses and stimulate healing in a way that nothing else does."

Martha found out that doctors have researched urine, too, using double-blind scientific studies and publishing their results in respected medical journals.

According to a 1954 issue of the *Journal of the American Medical Association*, medical journals had probably published more scientific papers about urine than about any other organic compound.

Researchers have discovered the effectiveness of urine therapy in illnesses ranging from AIDS to tuberculosis. At the Oxford Medical Symposium in 1981, Dr. N. Dunn told his allopathic colleagues that urine therapy had relieved multiple sclerosis, diabetes, lupus, rheumatoid arthritis, hepatitis, hypertension, pancreatic insufficiency and herpes.

So why, Martha wondered, doesn't anyone know about it? If your body produces a simple, clean, free substance that you can use to cure yourself of numerous diseases with no danger and no side effects, why isn't it being used?

Now Martha was on a mission. After a lifetime of misery, she had been healed, and she felt compelled to get the word out, explaining how urine therapy works and why you and I have never heard about it.

"I think that most of us are under the impression that somewhere in the sequestered halls of academia, benevolent doctors and research scientists are altruistically slaving over their petri dishes and test tubes, feverishly searching for new medical methods and cures that will relieve and eradicate physical suffering and illness—and that as soon as they make these wondrous new discoveries, they'll immediately release the results of their studies to a desperately expectant world of sick and suffering people," she wrote in her book.

And that's what she used to think—until she researched how it really works. She found out it can cost up to 150 million dollars to get a new drug approved. And she learned that drug companies are "the architects of today's medical system," because they finance most of today's medical research.

"Now, while the owners of these drug companies may have had some altruistic interests, the lifeblood of their companies was not medicine, but money," Martha wrote in her book. "It's in the drug industry's best interest to ignore and invalidate medicines and traditional therapies that can't be patented and don't produce big profits. And in simple economic terms, this is how any business survives and prospers—by selling and promoting the products that make the most money."

Martha Christy had looked into the medical monopoly and found that the companies in control aren't just promoting their own products, they've launched an all-out campaign to destroy any non-pharmaceutical product that works to heal illness—a sort of war on non-drugs.

Chapter 30

The thing that bugs me is that the people think the FDA is protecting them. It isn't. What the FDA is doing and what the public thinks it's doing are as different as night and day.
—Herbert Ley, MD,
Former FDA Commissioner

The War on Non-Drugs

When Whole Foods magazine surveyed herbal products retailers, asking what obstacles were in the way of increased herb sales, nearly half listed ways in which the medical monopoly manipulates information. Twenty-three percent pointed to the government restricting what type of information can be given to consumers, and eighteen percent said "scare stories" about herbs in the mainstream media. Another forty-one percent pointed to lack of consumer education; in other words, if people were made aware of the medical benefits of herbs, they would use them.

But they're not made aware, partly because the FDA has waged an all-out war on non-drugs. Just ask criminologist Elaine Feuer. When she turned her investigative skills toward the FDA, she discovered that it works diligently to protect the profits of big medicine. She learned that it prevents factual information from reaching the public and works to close companies that market alternatives. In her book, *Innocent Casualties: The FDA's War Against Humanity*, Feuer reports that the FDA seems to target those companies that offer remedies for the big money-making diseases, such as cancer and AIDS.

For these and other diseases, there's a long roster of inexpensive, highly effective cures hidden away from the public or labeled as snake oils.

The FDA's war on non-drugs has included many battles. In the 1970s, it tried to turn vitamin supplements into prescription drugs. After an uproar from the public, Congress rejected the idea that vitamins are so dangerous that they should only be prescribed by doctors.

"A variant of the process has already been successfully used to remove certain herbs from the shelves of stores. If you can't get an herb labeled as a drug, get it labeled a food additive. It can then be controlled by the bureaucrats in the FDA," writes pharmacologist Mowrey.

And if re-classifying herbs as drugs or food additives doesn't work, the FDA uses Orwellian tactics in its ongoing war. In 1990, for example, it tried to get a law passed that would have allowed it to make summary seizures of products from companies and tap telephone lines without a court warrant. Public pressure again defeated these strong-arm tactics.

In 1993, the FDA tried another tactic, seeking to classify all amino acids and many minerals as prescription drugs. The public outcry caused a backlash, and Congress passed the Dietary Supplement Health and Education Act in 1994 to limit the FDA's authority to regulate supplements.

Most recently, the FDA has been trying to go after Internet companies that sell herbs and other non-monopoly treatments. It is charging that these companies dispense drugs without a prescription.

In *The Assault on Medical Freedom*, author Joseph Lisa exposes previously secret documents from the medical industry to show that the FDA, the pharmaceuticals industry, insurance companies and the AMA work together to discredit natural medicine. He calls this collusion "medlock." The documents show how the FDA worked with the Pharmaceutical Advertising Council in 1983 to create the Public Service Anti-Quackery Campaign to make people think alternative remedies were useless snake oils. The FDA thus became the tool for the drug industry to violate antitrust laws by helping to close down companies that compete with pharmaceutical giants. The result, according to Lisa, is "nothing less than an enforced totalitarian medical-pharmaceutical police state."

But because herbs and vitamins are so effective, the public has protected its access to them. So the FDA, unable to gain control of all herbs and vitamins, has been targeting them one at a time, trying to prove their dangers. When that fails, the debunkers go into action, warning the public to avoid a substance because it has not been properly tested. When scientific, double-blind studies prove the effectiveness of these substances, the evidence is ignored.

Pharmacologist Mowrey went looking for studies on whether herbs offer effective cures and found that thousands of scientific studies have proven not only the effectiveness of herbs but that they often work as well as their synthetic copies.

Journalist Leviton found the same thing. "Clinical studies continue to build the case that dietary supplements and botanicals could be successfully used to manage if not reverse most diseases without the cost, toxicity, or side effects of conventional drugs," he writes. "The implications are obvious: Alternative medicine could bankrupt the pharmaceutical industry." As a result, he says, "Freedom of choice is available in most areas of American life except medicine."

Killing the Competition

And so the FDA acts as the drug industry's enforcement agency, pushing worthwhile natural medicines off the market. How, specifically, does it do this?

Mowrey tells the story of sassafras tea, a blood cleanser that has been used as a tonic in the United States for centuries. One of its constituents, safrole, can be toxic to the liver when extracted from the herb and administered in large doses. Like many herbs with toxic compounds, the whole plant contains other substances that neutralize the toxic one. No study had ever shown that the herb sassafras was toxic. There wasn't even anecdotal evidence that the tea posed a danger. But the FDA prohibited its interstate shipment in 1976 based on this reasoning: When sassafras (a food) is added to water (also a food), the substance safrole migrates from the sassafras into the water and therefore becomes a food additive.

Once this convoluted reasoning was used to label sassafras a food additive, the FDA was allowed to control it.

"During the entire proceedings, the power of the scientific method, initially utilized to create the controversy, became impotent in resolving the situation. Unasked questions cannot be answered. The question of whether whole sassafras herb or even sassafras tea was toxic to the liver was never experimentally addressed," Mowrey reported.

Sassafras tea is just one of a long list of healthful substances that U.S. consumers have been frightened away from.

Canadian scientist Gaston Naessens put together an herbal cancer remedy called 714-X. As of 1991, it had cured more than one thousand cancer patients and several AIDS patients. But as long as the medical monopoly remains, this safe cancer cure will not be used in the United States.

When Jason Winters cured his cancer with another herbal combination, he felt compelled to get the word out. "I must tell you that I was scared. I was not prepared to take on the billion-dollar drug companies, the medical associations and doctors, all of whom would chew up and spit out anyone that would dare to even say that possibly, just possibly, herbs can help," wrote Winters, whose book, *Killing Cancer*, has sold more than twelve million copies.

Winters outlines the typical fate of natural cancer and other cures that are advertised in U.S. publications: "Usually, the publication gets into a lot of trouble for printing it in the first place, then all future publicity is stopped. The persons selling the products are usually tricked or entrapped into a phony suit about 'practicing medicine without a license,' or if they can't stop them that way, they attack them on some income tax charge or other."

Those who practice natural medicine or sell natural remedies live with the knowledge that they could be closed down any day.

Self-healer Linda Koep, for example, is very careful about how she conducts business. After finding a combination of natural substances that cured her, she decided to represent the company that makes those products. Linda knows what will help those suffering from the symptoms she had, but without a medical license, she can't say so. The distributor from whom she was buying these substances was investigated by the FDA, so Koep is careful not to make any medical claims

Self-healer Kathy Stephens, a registered nurse, can't use the word "pain" when telling people how they can eliminate their pain. She must use the word "discomfort." Otherwise, she's making a medical claim.

Kathy suffered osteoarthritis pain for five years before her brother showed her a non-drug solution. The system of medicine in which she was trained offered only drugs and surgery. Her brother suggested she try magnets. "But being the professional nurse that I am, I laughed and scoffed," she recalls.

Then she went to a family reunion and camped out with her children.

Her brother set up her bed—a magnetic sleeping pad and pillow and a quilt containing far-infrared technology.

"The next morning, I opened my eyes and couldn't believe I had slept all night long. I moved around a little bit, and nothing hurt. I didn't have to push myself up with my hands to get out of the tent. I couldn't believe the difference it made in my body. I was so full of energy." She ordered a magnetic mattress that June day in 1999. Then she began selling the products that allow her to control her pain all day long.[1]

Kathy believes magnets can eliminate anyone's osteoarthritis pain. But she can't say so. Because she sells a non-monopoly product, she has lost the right of free speech.

It's not just the FDA that she has to worry about. The Federal Trade Commission in June 2001 announced it was cracking down on six dietary supplement companies. It claimed these companies were making false and potentially dangerous claims about products on the Internet. FTC admitted that neither it nor the FDA had received any reports of people injured by the products being sold. In fact, one of the products, the hormone DHEA, has been proven beneficial in studies conducted in allopathic labs. According to the *Townsend Letter for Doctors*, experimental results indicate that DHEA prevents some cancers, boosts the immune system, makes lab animals live longer and may reverse osteoporosis. Yet the FTC fined Oasis Wellness Network of Broomfield, Colorado, 150,000 dollars for claiming that a product containing DHEA can fight aging. It also ordered the company to restrict its advertising.

This would not have happened if one of the companies that belongs to the medical monopoly was selling the DHEA. But those companies don't bother to sell natural substances. They cannot patent—and therefore make huge profits—off natural substances. So they only make non-natural chemicals. And they use the federal government to keep natural substances from competing with them.

Winters sums up the system: "When a person is healing people but is not a medical doctor, does not belong to the AMA, and if he is not prescribing harmful drugs, then he can expect to be persecuted."

Self-healer Andrew Yachad contrasts the persecution of natural healers in the United States with the acceptance of alternative medicine in South Africa: "For example, this woman naturopath was operating a clinic in South Africa, and there was no equivalent of the AMA outside hauling her off to jail for witchcraft like they do in this country."

Self-healer Arlene Oostdyk says natural healers, to avoid prosecution, must avoid certain words, including "diagnosis," "disease" and "cure." She also says it's a shame that so many Americans have to leave the country to get effective treatment, and that so many physicians have to move to foreign soil to practice effective medicine. "A doctor who uses chelation has to go out of the country, and that's sick, because they're so persecuted," she says. "A lot of physicians would like to get into natural medicine, but they're worried about the persecution."

It makes you wonder how many Americans have suffered needlessly over the last half century, and how many have died unnecessarily. The larger question, perhaps, is what right does the government have to intervene in a person's medical decisions?

"There are cures out there, but our government and the pharmaceutical companies want control," says self-healer Sharon Rosa, a naturopath. "We do need medical doctors, but we need the Little-House-on-the-Prairie type, and the medical profession needs to allow people like me to practice, too."

Chapter 31

The results we obtained with thousands of patients of various races, sexes and ages with all types of cancer definitely prove Essiac to be a cure for cancer. Studies done in four laboratories in the United States and one more in Canada also fortify this claim.
—*Dr. Charles Brusch*
President Kennedy's personal physician

Suppressing Essiac

Another highly effective cancer cure, Essiac tea, has a tragic story that shows how the monopoly eliminates competition from natural healing substances. This story originates in Canada. A nurse there, Rene Caisse, had learned in 1922 that the Ojibwa (Chippewa) Indians brew together four plants—burdock, rhubarb, sheep sorrel and slippery elm—to rid the body of tumors and clean the blood. She began making the tea for cancer victims.

Eight doctors who saw Essiac's impact on one cancer patient asked the Canadian government to set up a clinic for Caisse. Instead, it threatened to arrest her. She stayed out of jail because she was not charging for the tea and was working under the supervision of physicians.

One of the physicians sent to investigate Caisse, Dr. W.C. Arnold, was so impressed with what he learned that he helped Caisse set up clinical trials. Cancer-ridden mice treated with Essiac lived fifty-two days longer than mice treated with other substances.

Individual physicians tried to help Caisse bring Essiac to the public, but the persecution from organized medicine was too severe. In 1930, the Canadian College of Physicians and Surgeons tried to have Caisse arrested for practicing medicine without a license. Once again, the fact that she was working under physicians saved her.

Threatened with imprisonment for the third time in 1932, Caisse requested a hearing with the minister of health, who reviewed the evidence and then allowed her to continue treating people with Essiac. Over the next eight years, she treated thousands of patients. Most had been labeled terminal by their doctors. After being treated with Essiac, more than eighty percent had their cancer disappear.

So successful was it, that more than 55,000 people signed a petition in 1938 asking the Ontario Parliament to let Caisse practice medicine in Ontario. The Canadian Medical Association and the Cancer Commission lobbied against the measure, and it failed by three votes.

Under continued persecution from the medical monopoly, Caisse had a nervous breakdown in 1942 and stopped treating patients. But the medical community didn't forget. The Cancer Commission wanted the formula for Essiac, and in 1958, Canada's premier asked Caisse to give it to them. She responded that she would do so only if the medical community acknowledged Essiac's efficacy and allowed cancer patients to take it. She was worried that otherwise, the monopoly would suppress the treatment.

The Cancer Institute would not agree to her conditions, and the standoff continued.

A year later, John F. Kennedy's personal physician, Dr. Charles Brusch, convinced the Sloan-Kettering Cancer Institute to test Essiac on animals. Initial tests showed Essiac worked, but the institute refused to continue testing unless Caisse divulged the formula. She would not. During the next two decades, Caisse tried to interest drug firms in Essiac, but they would not test it without the formula.

"Rene Caisse died in 1978 at the age of ninety. She spent a frustrating life trying to save people's lives with a simple herbal tea, only to have that effort thwarted by the politics and greed of the medical establishment," writes Cynthia Olsen, author of *Essiac: A Native Herbal Cancer Remedy*.

Eighty years after Caisse began using Essiac to treat cancer victims, the tea has finally reached the public, sold through health food stores and other outlets. Still, how many people have heard of it? Only a monopoly could suppress the public's awareness of a competing cancer treatment that has an eighty percent success rate with so-called terminal cancers.

*Step into a new world—a world
without chronic diseases.
Step out of your old world.
It has kept you a prisoner.
Try something new.*
**—Hulda Clark,
The Cure for All Diseases**

Chapter 32

Zeroing in on Zappers

Bioelectric medicine has been practiced since 46 A.D., when Greek phycians put electric eels in therapeutic foot baths and discovered they could reduce pain and improve circulation.

Doctors continued using electricity throughout the next two millennia, and by 1910, about half of all U.S. physicians used bioelectric medicine in their practices daily. That's when the Flexner Report came out. It listed both bioelectric medicine and nutritional counseling as invalid. Medical schools that taught either would no longer be funded. Why? The Flexner Report was financed by individuals whose fortunes were tied to pharmaceutical companies. And if people began using foods to maintain health and bioelectric devices to kill pathogens and shrink tumors, drug company profits would drop.

Today, the FDA has approved several bioelectric devices designed to reduce pain. But it continues to suppress those devices that can cure a wide range of diseases and that are inexpensive and therefore accessible to the general public without a visit to a doctor's office.

In the 1920s, Dr. Royal Raymond Rife invented the world's most powerful microscope and discovered that pathogens could be devitalized by beaming specific light frequencies at them. He also discovered that certain oscillation rates caused remissions in tumors. He built a frequency-generating machine and began studying which frequencies killed which pathogens.

In 1934, the University of Southen California assigned a team of physicians and pathologists to examine sixteen terminal cancer patients brought to Rife for treatment. The team concluded that fourteen of the patients were cancer-free after three months. For the other two, it took four months to be completely cured of cancer.

The American Medical Association, impressed with Rife's discoveries, tried to buy into the development and distribution rights to the new microscope and frequency generator. Rife declined the AMA's offer.

"Then, with hardly a pause, the AMA mounted a nasty suppressive campaign that eventually brought Rife to court with charges of illegal practice of medicine," medical journalist Leviton reports.

Rife and other researchers validating his data suddenly began having accidents. Rife's labs were destroyed by arson. Dr. Milbank Johnson, chairman of the research team assigned to examine the terminal cancer patients, died of poisoning, and his research papers were never found. Another physician who was duplicating Rife's studies was killed in a mysterious fire. Again, all the research papers disappeared.

Today, Africa's medical system has approved clinical use of the Rife frequency generator. But it remains illegal in the United States. Here, the lay public has taken over the research. Hundreds of people are spending between five hundred and three thousand dollars to buy or build their own Rife frequency generators. They're joining Internet discussion groups to discuss which frequencies work for which ailments.

In the next section of this book, you'll read about self-healer Jeff Houck's use of a Rife machine to rid himself of infectious organisms.

The Beck and Clark Zappers

The Beck zapper is another bioelectric medical device initially invented by doctors and now in the hands of the general public. Both Rife's and Beck's machines are effective against a wide range of diseases, but while the Rife frequency generator is particularly good at killing cancer, the Beck zapper is particularly good at eliminating AIDS.

Scientists at the Albert Einstein College of Medicine in New York discovered in 1990 that a very small electrical current could alter the outer protein layers of HIV in a way that stopped it from binding to receptor sites.[1] They filed patent number 5,139,684 for a machine that takes blood out of the body and electrifies it before putting it back in. Physicist Robert Beck of the University of California made the technology affordable and accessible to all, creating a small device that electrifies the blood without taking it out of the body. The machine includes two electrodes that are placed on the skin directly over the wrist or ankle arteries.

Dr. Beck left the country to test it on people with viral diseases. Although his test subjects seemed cured, some of them became re-infected by the same virus a year or two later. Beck discovered that his zapper worked only on viruses in the bloodstream, and if the virus remained in the lymph fluid, it could re-infect the blood. Beck built a second device called the magnetic pulser to reach viruses in the lymph system.

He decided not to profit from his devices, but rather to make them available to all. He published the schematics, parts list and instructions so that anyone could build the zapper and magnetic pulser for about seventy-five dollars and administer their own treatment at home.

He was harassed by the FDA, and his home was raided. But, until his death in 2002, he continued to lecture and write about the potential of bioelectric medicine to cure a wide range of diseases.

Self-healer Annie Wilkin used the Beck zapper as part of her self-treatment protocol.

Hulda Clark, a naturopath who holds a doctorate in physiology, promotes use of another kind of zapper in which the electricity enters the body through acupuncture points. She, too, published a parts list and diagrams for building the zapper so that anyone could make one. This inexpensive device, powered by a nine-volt battery, is used by holding copper rods in the hands. It devitalizes parasites and other pathogens.

Clark is a favorite target of the quack busters, not because her zapper is more effective than Beck's or Rife's, but because she's been very effective at getting the word out. She has published four books that can be found in most health food stores.

In 1999, the FBI arrested her for practicing medicine without a license. She was seventy years old at the time. Hundreds of people who have been helped by her methods joined together to work for her release. Six months later, the charges were dropped. Clark now operates a clinic in Mexico.

Self-healer Kim Dunn used the Clark zapper as one of the items in her treatment portfolio.

It's indisputable that homeopathy works; the fact that scientists can't prove how is basically their epistemological problem.
—Richard Leviton

Chapter 33

Halting Homeopathy

Homeopathy as a word is the opposite of allopathy. It's a system of medicine in which diseases are treated with minute doses of substances that create the same symptoms from which the patient is suffering.

In 1844, homeopaths formed the first national medical society in the United States, the American Institute of Homeopathy. Two years later, allopaths formed the American Medical Association.

The AMA of that day worked hard to corner the health-care market, excluding physicians who posed even the slightest threat to the formation of an allopathic monopoly. Doctors were kicked out of professional associations for serving on health boards that contained homeopaths or making a purchase at a homeopathic pharmacy. One physician lost his membership simply by discussing a patient with his wife, who was a homeopathist.

When the Flexner Report was issued, standardizing physician training, the homeopathic medical schools began closing. The once strong profession, with fifteen thousand practitioners and twenty schools in the United States, almost disappeared from the nation. By 1940, all of the homeopathic medical colleges in the United States had closed.

In other countries without a medical monopoly, homeopathy never faltered. In India—where Mahatma Gandhi once said that homeopathy cures a greater number of people than any other method—there are one hundred and twenty homeopathic medical schools and more than 100,000 practitioners.

So effective is homeopathy that the AMA could never completely eliminate it. A few American practitioners kept practicing, and in recent years, homeopathy's popularity has been revived, particularly among naturopathic physicians.

Homeopathy has passed the double-blind-test standard and been proven effective.

In 1988, scientists in France, Canada, Italy and Israel together conducted studies using homeopathic doses of antibodies to see if they would make white blood cells react. They replicated their results in seventy experiments, showing that homeopathic dilutions work. They published their results in *Nature*, Britain's top scientific journal.

But the journal's editors couldn't believe that a tiny dose containing no molecular traces of a substance could be biologically active. The results, said the journal, contradict the very basis upon which science has rested for two hundred years. So the journal debunked the seventy scientific experiments with a very unscientific investigation.

Nature editor John Maddox went to the Paris lab with magician debunker James Randi and a non-scientist from the National Institutes of Health. This team watched the experiment replicated seven times, then declared that it was a hoax. It never explained how the hoax was accomplished, but *Nature* published a retraction of the original article about the efficacy of homeopathy.

In the chapter about quantum physics, we'll see how the most modern developments in science help explain how homeopathy works. The medical community's refusal to believe it works is much like scientists in the 1500s refusing to believe that the earth rotates around the sun, even after it had been proven mathematically.

The time has come for
ushering in an era of balance
between the synthetic and the natural.
—Daniel Mowrey

Chapter 34

The End of the Beginning

T he health-care monopoly that has held a stranglehold on American medicine for nearly a century is loosening its grip.

"Health care consumers today are witnessing and experiencing first-hand the collapse of a medical system based on profit and saturated with the mistaken assumption that manmade drugs can be guaranteed to be safe and can completely usurp the healing power of nature," says self-healer Martha Christy.

Three factors have been slowly coming together that eventually will lead to a health-care system that is holistic, effective and affordable. These factors began to show up as early as the 1920s, and the twenty-first century will see the beginning of a new medical system in America.

The first two factors are exactly the same things that allowed allopathy to gain its monopoly: capitalism and scientific reductionism. These two factors are now contributing to the monopoly's demise.

In a capitalistic society, consumers have power, and they will not continue to buy a bad medical product if a better one is available.

Scientific reductionism led scientists to reduce nature to the smallest parts they could find, and the new science of those smallest parts—called quantum physics—shows the flaws in allopathy's most basic beliefs. Allopathy is no longer scientifically sound.

We'll discuss these two factors in more depth before this section ends. But first, let's take a look at the third factor that is ushering in the new era. That factor is the rise in chronic illness.

*The epidemic of chronic illness
in the United States,
particularly arterial disease
and cancer, is the stellar
embarrassment of medicine
and its high-technology weapons.*
—Joseph Beasely, MD
The Betrayal of Health

Chapter 35

The Kink in
Allopathy's Armor

A 1996 study by University of California at San Francisco shows the extent of America's health-care crisis. It found that 100 million Americans have a chronic illness or disability. That's about one in every three Americans. Here's what else the researchers reported:

- The chronically ill and their insurance providers spend 425 billion dollars a year on doctors, hospitals and medication.
- The chronically ill account for eighty-three percent of prescription drug use, eighty percent of hospitalizations, sixty-six percent of physician visits, fifty-five percent of emergency room visits, and ninety-six percent of professional home care.
- One in every four people younger than eighteen has at least one chronic ailment, while one in three people age eighteen to forty-four is chronically ill, and sixty-six percent of people ages forty-five to sixty-four suffer from a chronic illness.
- The number of chronically ill is expected to swell to 150 million by 2030.

Allopaths describe chronic conditions as those that affect people for more than three months. But the simpler definition of chronic illness is this: An illness that doctors don't know how to cure.

"The allopathic system is the best trauma and critical care system in the world. But it doesn't even begin to address chronic illnesses, and that's where most people are sick," says self-healer Jeff Houck.

153

Chronic conditions have grown exponentially due to the industrialization of America, which has resulted in an environment saturated with chemicals. We breathe carbon dioxide in our air, eat pesticides in our foods and drink bleach in our water. Add the stress of modern life, and the body's systems are bound to break down.

When they do, doctors schooled in the one-agent-one-disease theory of medicine don't know what to do. They're divided into specialties and can't deal with a system-wide problem. They're not used to looking at the body holistically, nor do they consider the mind's impact on it. So they do not have the tools to deal with chronic illness. They have no answers, because they focus only on treating symptoms, but the problem usually originates with an underlying system failure.

"The main reason for the failure of modern medical science is that it is dealing with results and not causes." That's what Dr. Edward Bach wrote back in the early 1900s, before chronic illness reached epidemic proportions.

Since then, we have not only experienced dramatic rises in cancer, heart disease and other chronic killers, we've also seen the outbreak of AIDS and other immune diseases.

"AIDS is the cul-de-sac at the end of the allopathic paradigm," says medical journalist Leviton. "It's not a question of which specific virus triggers what condition, but that the immune system as the heart of human organic integrity is radically compromised."

AIDS, cancer, arthritis, chronic fatigue syndrome, allergies—all include the component of a compromised immune system. So what do medical doctors use to treat them? Immune-damaging drugs and surgeries.

"Conventional biomedicine—so strikingly successful in the treatment of overwhelming infection, surgical and medical emergencies, and congenital defects—has not only been unable to stem the tide of (chronic) conditions... It has, in attempting to treat them, produced a host of destructive side effects," writes James S. Gordon, clinical professor of psychiatry and family medicine at Georgetown University Medical School, in *Manifesto for a New Medicine.*

The damage done by allopathic treatments is proof enough that MDs do not have the correct tools to cure disease. And because they do not have the right tools and knowledge, they fail to make Americans healthier.

"The best estimates are that the medical system (doctors, drugs, hospitals) affects about ten percent of the usual indices for measuring health," according to Aaron Wildavsky, former dean of the Graduate School of Public Policy at the University of California at Berkeley.

Because they have no impact on the other ninety percent, allopaths resign themselves to accepting chronic illnesses as inevitable and incurable. They provide pills for pain, but they do not fully understand its pathways. They create chemicals to kill cancer cells, but they cannot stop its causes. They tell us that science will come up with the answers, but it doesn't.

Today, Americans are suffering from mostly the same common major diseases that were prevalent in the 1950s. Since then, the medical world has created a tremendous body of knowledge about the diseases, but not a single cure. We continue to hear about research "breakthroughs" that could lead to future cures. But they never pay off. The cure doesn't come.

And Americans are beginning to ask why.

"After all these billions of dollars we're pouring into medical research, why is there more chronic illness? Why are more kids coming up with leukemia? Now they have a childhood arthritis. Doesn't anyone say the emperor's not wearing any clothes?" asks self-healer Andrew Yachad.

The answer is yes. People are seeing the weaknesses of allopathic medicine. Chronic illness is showing the kink in allopathy's armor. People are sick and tired of being sick and tired. They're frustrated by doctors who can neither diagnose nor cure them.

Dissatisfied and Disillusioned

Listen to the story of Michael Romano, age eighty-five, diagnosed with prostate cancer in the mid 1990s:

"They gave me radiation, but it started coming back, so they gave me hormones, and that dropped my numbers way down like a brick. But the side effects were bad. So last time I went to the prostate doctor, I said, the numbers are down, let's not give me any more shots of hormones for awhile. He said okay.

"Then I came up with non-Hodgkin's lymphoma after the prostate cancer. It was on my neck, and they carved it out. Then they gave me radiation. It had side effects, like bad tooth decay. The lymphoma came back again. This time I diagnosed it myself, but the doctor confirmed it. He carved it out again and gave me chemo. The side effects weren't too bad.

"I had shortness of breath, and I'm looking for answers. I'm taking a drug for glaucoma, and that may be the culprit, but I can't stop that, because I don't want to go blind. So I ask the doctors why I have shortness of breath and no one has any answers. So I gave up on all the doctors. If they can't answer me, I've got to go look for answers myself.

"I'm a little bit disillusioned with the doctors. That's why I took the (Essiac) tea. I was worried the hormones were causing shortness of breath, and the doctors couldn't tell me whether it was. They didn't know. I'm disillusioned with jokers who tell me, 'I don't know what it is.'"

He's not the only one.

Many people, after going from doctor to doctor for chronic conditions and finding no answers, are giving up on doctors. They are beginning to question whether the doctor's medicine really is best. They are turning to whatever alternatives they can find and discovering that many alternative practitioners have the answers. Not only do they offer cures, they do so without invasive surgeries and toxic drugs.

"As we watch the often terrible and fatal consequences of decades of complete reliance on immune-suppressing synthetic drugs and surgical techniques unfold, we worriedly search the pages of history to rediscover and relearn the lost arts of caring for ourselves with simple, safe, and healthful natural healing," says self-healer Martha Christy.

We're beginning to search for those simple healing methods because allopathy has failed to cure chronic illness. That failure is the first of three factors leading to a new medicine for the future.

Why is alternative medicine's
popularity growing so rapidly?
Because it works, is affordable
and doesn't fill your life
with side effects.
—*Richard Leviton*

Chapter 36

Buyer, Be Aware

The second factor leading to a new medicine of the future is capitalism. You'll recall our discussion of how a capitalistic society works. It's based on this assumption: If people are allowed to pursue their self-interest by producing and selling goods in a self-regulating marketplace, it will result in the well-being of society, because businesses will be forced by competition to use their resources in ways that satisfy consumers.

Capitalism is a self-adjusting system. So in spite of allopathic medicine's success in establishing a monopoly, it is not permanent. If the monopoly's product does not satisfy the consumer, the consumer will stop buying it. The capitalistic system eventually will prevail. It's beginning to do so right now.

Statistics show widespread dissatisfaction with medicine's current product. A survey of thirty-seven thousand patients at one hundred and twenty hospitals and clinics showed that about one-third felt poorly prepared to return home, experienced trouble getting basic medical questions answered and felt they had too little input in decisions affecting their treatment.[1] More than half of all patients are concerned about the potential side effects of prescribed medications.[2]

One of the biggest indictments of the allopathic industry was a survey conducted by Standford University in 1998. It shocked the medical community by showing just how disappointed consumers are with allopathic products. It found that nearly seventy percent of Americans had turned to unconventional medical therapies, and one in three did so on a regular basis.

In the past, physicians had been able to hamper the growth of alternative medicine by calling it quackery and warning their patients away from it. But patients were no longer giving their doctors that opportunity. According to a 1997 survey published in *Archives of Family Medicine*, fifty-three percent of the people using alternative medicine do not tell their family doctors about it.

Where did the medical establishment go wrong? It had been controlling medical school curricula, research and government regulation for decades. Why could it not also control its patients?

First, those patients were paying more and more. Whenever a product's cost increases exponentially, consumers begin considering their purchase decisions more carefully. Consumers Union, which publishes *Consumer Reports* magazine, reported in 1996 that more than 2.5 million families spent thirty percent or more of their earnings on health care. Even the insured spent a lot: Nine million families with medical insurance coverage spent more than ten percent of their household income on health care.

Second, those people noticed that the product often didn't work very well, yet the "seller" didn't offer refunds or warranties. Consumer dissatisfaction grew.

Third, a new health and fitness market sprang up, touting the idea that people could take responsibility for their physical well-being. In the late 1970s, a noticeable number of people began educating themselves about their health. Health clubs sprang up in every town. Vitamin sales skyrocketed. Organic food became a fad. And the term "preventive medicine" became a buzzword.

And thus, some consumers began reclaiming their power. They first took health maintenance—and then disease treatment—into their own hands. Dissatisfied with the results they got from allopathy, they began searching for other options. The information age empowered them to do their own research. The Internet made research easy. It presented the information in layman's terms.

So the customer was dissatisfied with the product and had the ability to look for a different product. When he found the alternative product, he discovered that it cost much less and worked just as well or better. No wonder it took less than a decade for the number of alternative health users in the United States to double.

Signs of a Weakening Monopoly

Evidence of the allopathic monopoly's impending breakup can be seen in the growth of the natural health products market, the growing number of alternative health practitioners, and in new government laws that open up access to alternative health. You can also see the return to holistic medicine in the insurance industry's increasing willingness to cover holistic treatments and the allopathic world's sudden willingness to include some natural health methods in its repertoire of offerings.

The first sign of a weakening monopoly is the rise of competing products. Trade magazines such as *Natural Foods Merchandiser* frequently report annual sales of herbs and dietary supplements growing at rates ranging from sixteen to thirty-three percent a year.

The second sign of a weakening medical monopoly is the rise of non-monopoly practitioners. For example, only one hundred and fifty homeopathists practiced in the United States in 1970. By the late 1990s, that number was up to three thousand, and about a third of those are medical doctors. The per capita supply of alternative practitioners is expected to grow 124 percent between 1994 and 2010, while the number of conventional doctors grows by just sixteen percent.[3]

The third sign of a weakening medical monopoly is government action to allow competition from non-monopoly service providers. As more and more people have discovered the efficacy of natural medicine, patient grassroots campaigns have mobilized to create freedom of choice in medical treatment, and governments have responded. When Congress debated the Access to Medical Treatment Act in 1998, it considered allowing any practitioner to offer any treatment that is not harmful. Although that federal legislation didn't pass, state governments have been slowly opening the way for alternative medicine to be practiced legally. During the 1990s, eight states passed laws that protect medical doctors who use alternative therapies. The number of states licensing naturopaths is increasing, and by the beginning of 2002, it was up to twelve. Acupuncturists are now licensed in thirty-four states, and eleven states mandate that health plans cover chiropractic care.

Minnesota recently became the first state to authorize the practice of non-allopathic medicine by unlicensed practitioners. The Complementary and Alternative Health Care, Freedom of Access Act allows herbalists, naturopaths, acupressure practitioners and more than a dozen alternative therapists to offer their services without fear of prosecution. The law says alternative practitioners may not provide medical diagnoses or recommend clients stop using doctor-prescribed treatment. In addition, alternative practitioners must provide clients with a "client bill of rights" that directs them to complain to the Minnesota Department of Health if they are not satisfied with the practitioner's services.

Washington State's legislature also has been progressive in responding to the consumer rush to holistic medicine. In 1996, it became the first to tell insurers they must pay for non-allopathic care—even if it's considered "fringe"—as long as the treatment is offered by a licensed or certified health-care practitioner.

That brings us to the fourth sign of a weakening monopoly: The people who hold the purse strings—the insurers—begin to include non-monopoly services.

Oxford Health Plans made a big media splash in 1996 when it began covering alternative therapies. The move was so unusual that *Money* magazine, the *New York Times* and the *Wall Street Journal* all covered it. According to the company's senior vice president, David Snow, the company's decision was based on customer demand. The insurer had surveyed its 1.4 million members and found thirty-three percent had used alternative care the prior year. The company's chief executive, Stephen Wigging, added that Oxford also took into consideration the fact that alternative treatments are much less expensive.

Since then, other insurance companies have begun looking at the potential for larger clientele and smaller treatment bills if they include alternative medicine in their coverage plans. A 1999 report by Landmark Healthcare showed sixty-seven percent of HMOs now offer at least one form of alternative medicine.

Doctors React to the Trend

After patients, governments and insurers began shifting toward acceptance of holistic health care, one more group had yet to react to the trend: the physicians themselves. But now, even they are getting in on the act.

They initially took notice when a 1993 study by Dr. David Eisenberg was published. It shocked the medical community, because it showed the deep and widespread dissatisfaction with allopathy. The study found that in 1990, Americans made about 425 million visits to unconventional health-care providers, compared to 388 million visits to primary care physicians. And they spent 13.7 billion dollars on unconventional therapies, three-quarters of which was paid out of pocket.[4]

Eisenberg's follow-up study, published in 1998, showed a forty-seven percent increase in total visits to alternative medicine practitioners, up to 629 million visits in 1997. And patients were now spending 21.2 billion dollars a year for these alternative treatments.[5]

"These facts alarmed allopathic doctors, because for decades they have been institutionally and professionally aligned against such deviations from therapeutic norms," says medical journalist Leviton. "They had vig-orously promoted the public view that holistic, complementary, empiric and natural medicines were just inches short of unscientific quackery. Now, a statistical study published in their own peer review journal was telling them their patients thought differently and were willing to pay for their rebellious thoughts too."

Other reports in medical journals showed that it was the high-end customers who were dissatisfied with allopathic products and services. *The New England Journal of Medicine*, for example, reported that the biggest consumers of alternative medicine were comparatively well-off, well-educated people ages twenty-five to forty-nine. When the market segment that can best afford your products and services decides to shop elsewhere, you sit up and take notice.

The AMA began responding to the threat in 1995, when it issued a statement that advised its 300,000 members to learn about alternative treatments.

The federal government also took notice. Congress told the National Institutes of Health to establish an Office of Alternative Medicine, and it, too, began looking into the treatments that were eating away at allopathy's monopoly. It found that eighty percent of medical students want training in alternative therapies. The medical schools responded. In a drastic turn-about, two-thirds of medical schools now offer classes on complementary and alternative medicine, and thirty-one percent of those courses are required.

Sensing they could be in danger of losing their very livelihoods, those already out of medical school have begun suggesting that their patients use alternative therapies and products. In a 2000 survey by Health Products Research, Inc., fifty percent of 3,200 doctors surveyed said they expect to start recommending or increase their recommendations for homeopathic and holistic treatments over the next year.

There are now many examples of allopathic medical establishments offering complementary and alternative medicine. At the University of Pittsburgh Medical Center, psychiatrists now prescribe herbal medicines for depression. Beth Israel Medical Center in New York City has opened a specialized Center for Health and Healing, where physicians work alongside chiropractors, homeopathists and other alternative practitioners.

But one big question remains: Will allopathy accept alternative medicine, or will it usurp it?

Chiropractors are already expressing concern that physicians with just a bit of chiropractic training are doing spinal adjustments, and not very effectively. They're worried that patients will think they don't need to go to a chiropractor since a physician offers the service.

The suspicion that allopathy may simply be trying to usurp alternative medicine—co-opt it to gain control of it—is not mere paranoia. The drug industry has been trying for years to either eliminate or gain control of herbal medicines. And its motivation is not altruistic.

"If herbs continue to be marketed and used in spite of the unproven quackery stigma, there is another method available for ridding them from the marketplace: Admit that herbs work, admit that they have potent properties, and then label them drugs" so that only pharmaceutical companies can sell them, says pharmacist Mowrey. In fact, the FDA, acting as the enforcement arm of the pharmaceutical industry, has been trying to do just that.

But it hasn't worked. At least not yet. And the reason it hasn't is because capitalism is truly a self-regulating system. The consumer is king. The consumer eventually gets what the consumer wants. When that happens, we won't have a strictly allopathic system suppressing natural medicine. Nor will we have a natural-health system controlled by allopaths.

We'll have some sort of combination that's the most effective in address-ing the health-care needs of American medical consumers.

The allopathic approach will commingle with alternative medicine to produce a broader medical system that encompasses both natural cures that work so well for chronic illness and space-age technologies that work so well for acute conditions. Imagine a combined medicine in which an-cient knowledge is combined with high-tech advances.

If capitalism continues to modify the medical marketplace, we'll have the best of both worlds. The only question is when.

To reincorporate the notion of healing
into the theory and practice of medicine,
medical science will have to transcend
its narrow view of health and illness.
This does not mean that it will
have to be less scientific.
On the contrary, by broadening
its conceptual basis,
it will become more consistent with
recent developments in modern science.
— Fritjof Capra

Chapter 37

From Quackery
to Cutting Edge

We've just seen how the capitalistic system that allowed allopathy's monopoly is also helping to end that monopoly. In the same way, the mechanistic and reductionist science that led to allopathy will also lead beyond it.

Medicine is not static. It changes based on our level of knowledge. It stagnates when we're stuck with limited theories. It advances again when our understanding expands.

After four hundred years using limited theories, we're on the verge of a new understanding. Let's take a look at how we got there.

Before Descartes put forth the theory that the universe worked like a big machine, medicine operated in a more holistic fashion. Health-care practitioners looked not only at the physical mechanisms causing disease, they also looked at the patient's social environment and spiritual state. They understood the interplay between mind and body and treated the whole person.

But then the mechanistic worldview penetrated medicine. Mind and body became separate. The doctor became a mechanic, manipulating the physical parts instead of healing the whole system. The very concept of healing got lost. The body became a machine that could be analyzed in terms of its parts. Disease was caused by a malfunctioning of biological mechanisms. The doctor simply had to fix the malfunctioning part.

First, he had to find it, and to do so required studying all the parts of the body machine, all the way down to the smallest. The doctor had to understand the systems that made up the body, such as the circulatory and nervous systems. Then he had to understand the organs that made up the systems, then the tissues that made up the organs. Looking at ever smaller parts, he studied the cells that made up the tissues, the parts of the cell, and the molecules that made up those parts.

The problem is, all this knowledge about molecules, cells, tissues and organs didn't give doctors the knowledge to cure disease. It left one-third of Americans with chronic or deadly illnesses that doctors are powerless to cure.

By concentrating on smaller and smaller parts, allopathy lost sight of the human being behind the disease, and the concept of healing was tossed out. Healing processes could not be measured or explained in terms of science. For example, the doctor could tell you the physiological process that causes the blood to clot to start closing a wound, but he could not tell you what makes it decide to clot or why the tissue chooses to reform. Whatever that thing is, it can't yet be measured and quantified, so it's not considered scientific. Without a scientific explanation, the concept of healing must be discarded.

Those who consider themselves scientific are working with a science so limited that they can figure out how various physical mechanisms works, but not why. For example, scientists now understand the structure of DNA, but they don't know why dividing cells with identical genetic information specialize into different tissues—muscles, bones nerves. As physicist Capra puts it, "Biologists know the alphabet of the genetic code but have almost no idea of its syntax."

Human ecologist Rene Dubos points out that this leads to the ridiculous situation of science refusing to study life itself. Life cannot be explained in reductionist terms. As a result, biologists usually feel most at ease when the thing they are studying is no longer alive, Dubos says in *Man, Medicine and Environment*.

"Biologists are busy dissecting the human body down to its minute components, and in doing so are gathering an impressive amount of knowledge about its cellular and molecular mechanisms, but they still do not know how we breathe, regulate our body temperature, digest, or focus our attention," he says. "They know some of the nervous circuits, but most of the integrative actions remain to be understood. The same is true of the healing of wounds, and the nature and pathways of pain also remain largely mysterious."

And yet we expect them to figure out how to cure cancer and diabetes. No wonder the world's most modern medicine is such a dismal failure when it comes to chronic illness.

Fortunately, the same reductionist thinking that led to these limitations will also allow medical science to go beyond these limitations. By outlining the scientific method, Descartes created a way for those who came after him to discover his mistakes.

Science just had to get a bit smaller.

The Smallest Science

When scientists concluded that they could learn the most about physical bodies by studying their parts, then the parts of those parts, and so on, they were on the right track. The problem is, until recently, our measuring devices could only observe things so small and no smaller. To develop a truly effective medicine, doctors just have to take the next step. They have to look at the particles that make up the atoms that make up the molecules that make up the cells that make up the tissues that make up the organs that make up the systems that make up the body.

Quantum physicists have already done that. And what they've discovered challenges the basic concepts that have guided medicine for more than four centuries. When scientists peered into the world of electrons, protons, muons and quarks, what they discovered shook the foundation of their beliefs.

These scientists—quantum physicists such as Albert Einstein—suddenly had to consider the possibility that nature did not follow mechanistic laws after all. Reduced to its most minute level, it behaved more like a thought than a machine. This was a revolutionary discovery. And it will take time for it to permeate medicine.

Previous scientific revolutions had brought about drastic changes in concepts of how the universe worked, but it took many years for the new concepts to take hold. In the 1500s, scientists firmly believed that the sun revolved around the Earth. They were flat wrong, and Galileo proved it. But his contemporaries refused to look through his telescope, because they were afraid to see something that might contradict their truth. It took decades for Galileo to announce his findings, and decades more for it to become accepted as the new truth.

It may take even longer for quantum physics to replace the old worldview. Old-time scientists may have been reluctant to accept that the earth revolved around the sun, but at least they could imagine it. Quantum discoveries, on the other hand, are not so easily imaginable.

In quantum physics, the new reality is described in the language of mathematics, and it seems to make no sense at all. The tiniest bits of matter contain no matter whatsoever. One particle of matter can co-exist simultaneously in two locations. A tiny piece of an object contains the blueprint for the entire object. Solid objects are not solid.

"Every time they (physicists) asked nature a question in an atomic experiment, nature answered with a paradox," explains Capra.

Now, after a century of exploration, physicists have begun adjusting to the quantum reality, and it will become the basis of a new medicine. It will allow medical science to transcend its limited view of healing. It will explain how the theories underlying alternative medicine are scientifically valid.

Fortunately, physicists such as Capra have been translating quantum concepts into layman's terms. And a few doctors, such as Deepak Chopra —an endocrinologist whose books include *Quantum Healing: Exploring the Frontiers of Mind Body Medicine*—are already applying those concepts to medicine.

And just as it took a creative thinker like Galileo and a century of time to fully shatter the geocentric worldview, it will take time for today's new science to permeate the minds of doctors and their patients.

When it does, the so-called quackery of today will become the cutting edge medicine of tomorrow.

*Scientists will not need to be reluctant to
adopt a holistic framework...
for fear of being unscientific.
Modern physics can show them
that such a framework
is not only scientific
but is in agreement with
the most advanced scientific theories
of physical reality.*
—*Fritjof Capra*

Chapter 38

Quantum Medicine

et's discuss briefly some of the discoveries in this most modern science of quantum physics to show how it supports some alternative therapies. Wave-particle duality, the properties of electromagnetic fields, the holographic effect, the impact of the observer—these discoveries can help explain how homeopathy cures, why the holistic approach is so effective, how Reiki and Qigong can heal tissues, what makes iridology an effective diagnostic tool, why placebos work about thirty percent of the time.

For many years, we have had the tools to test alternative therapies and show that they work. But we never had the scientific understanding to explain why they work. So we pretended they didn't.

Remember this when your doctor tells you something is unscientific. He may simply mean the science he has learned is not yet advanced enough to explain it. Quantum science may explain it. Your doctor just didn't take that class.

Let's look at the development of quantum physics before we see which of its discoveries explain the efficacy of various non-allopathic treatments.

In the nineteenth century, scientists began studying electric and magnetic phenomena. Physicists such as Michael Faraday and Clerk Maxwell had soon replaced Isaac Newton's old idea of forces with the new idea of force fields. They showed that fields had a reality separate from the bodies upon which they acted. In other words, gravity didn't need an apple.

The theory of electrodynamics was thus born. It enabled physicists to discover the nature of light. They learned that light is a rapidly alternating electromagnetic field traveling through space in the form of waves.

Early twentieth century physicists moved the science forward, developing relativity theory and quantum theory. They discovered that the very building blocks of nature are not made of solid particles but of light waves.

Einstein's famous equation, $E=mc^2$ (energy equals mass times the speed of light squared), showed that mass—solid objects, including the physical body—is nothing but a form of energy.

To add confusion to this confounding discovery, the new physicists then discovered that light particles are solid, too. This was called wave-particle duality. But how can an atomic particle—a piece of an atom, such as an electron—be both a solid object and a non-solid wave? When observed in one way, it has the characteristics of being solid. When observed in another way, it has the characteristics of being an electromagnetic wave. To explain this, physicist Niels Bohr coined the term "complementarity," saying both descriptions complement each other by describing the same reality.

Then physicists discovered these waves were organized into unified fields. Solid matter—including the physical body—was now "a complicated web of relations between the various parts of a unified field," as Capra describes it.

Physicist David Bohm postulated that everything in the universe is part of an "unbroken wholeness." He points to the properties of a hologram, in which each part of the projected image contains the whole image. In other words, if you have a holographic negative of an apple and shine light through just a tiny part of the stem, the image of the entire apple will show up in the hologram.

Another thing scientists discovered in the quantum world was that cause-and-effect no longer applies. An electron may jump from one atomic orbit to another without a single event causing it. The dynamics of the system—its connection to the whole—determine the probability, but not the certainty, that the electron will jump from one orbit to another. Thus was born probability theory.

Quantum physicists also discovered that an objective experiment was impossible; the very fact of observing the experiment changes its outcome. In fact, observation determines the very properties of what is being observed.

"The crucial feature of quantum theory is that the observer is not only necessary to observe the properties of an atomic phenomenon, but is necessary even to bring about these properties," Capra explains. "The electron does not have objective properties independent of my mind. In atomic physics, the sharp Cartesian division between mind and matter, between the observer and the observed, can no longer be maintained."

Because mind impacts matter, objective scientific truth is impossible to come by. This is called the uncertainty principle.

So how does this relate to medicine and healing?

First, the unbroken wholeness of matter calls for a holistic approach to medicine. Imagine if an oncologist understood that the dynamics of the whole human system determined the probability that cells would mutate into cancer. He would no longer look for a single causative factor nor for one silver-bullet chemical to treat it.

If he understood how mind moves matter, he might avoid pronouncing a death sentence and instead affirm the patient's ability to heal even a malignant tumor. He might suggest the patient think the cancer away.

Thinking entails electrical and chemical processes and therefore can cause physical changes, writes Blair Justice in *Who Gets Sick*. Quantum physics will allow doctors to see the science behind this statement.

From the perspective of most modern-day physicians, homeopathy doesn't make sense. If a substance is so dilute with water that no chemical trace of the substance remains, how can that impact the body? The quantum physicist answers: The water still contains the energy imprint of the substance. Its impact is just as intense as the chemical impact. Energy and matter are one and the same. Homeopathists have been saying for two centuries that disease symptoms are the body's way of responding to vibratory distortions. We finally have the science to back that statement up.

"By giving a remedy which resembles the disease, the instinctive vital force is compelled to increase its vital energy until it becomes stronger than the disease, which, in turn, is vanquished." That statement, written by Samuel Hahnemann in homeopathy's definitive text, *Organon of Medicine,* cannot be imagined by the physician but is easily accepted by the physicist.

Since matter—the physical body and its organs and tissues—are made of electro-magnetic waves, it is no wonder that homeopathy works. And it becomes evident why energy-based healing systems, such as Reiki and Qigong, are effective, and why the use of bioelectric devices, such as zappers and the Rife machine, makes sense.

"In Reiki, until recently, they couldn't harness a person to a machine and see the differences. The ability to measure energy flow is just recent," says self-healer Jeff Houck, a Reiki practitioner.

The quantum principle of nonlocality fits perfectly with acupuncture. And the principles of the hologram explain why alternative diagnostic techniques such as iridology work: One small part contains the diagram of the whole.

If the physical world operates more like a thought than a machine, then the placebo effect, which has baffled scientists for generations, is perfectly scientific. Suddenly, it becomes a powerful tool in healing rather than an experimental nuisance.

Of course, the uncertainty principle makes double-blind tests useless. The fact that the observer impacts the outcome of what he is observing makes all so-called scientific experiments very unscientific indeed. The only truly double-blind experiment would be one that was not observed at all.

"Every contemporary physicist (agrees) that modern physics has transcended the mechanistic Cartesian view of the world and is leading us to a holistic and intrinsically dynamic conception of the universe," Capra says.

This holistic view will one day permeate medicine. The reductionist philosophy that led us into allopathic folly will lead us to a new medicine in which healing is understood and "cure" is not a dirty word.

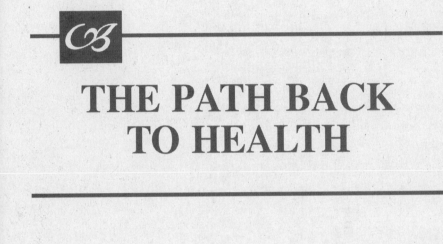

THE PATH BACK
TO HEALTH

I took the road less traveled by,
and that has made all the difference.
—Robert Frost

Chapter 39

The Path Less Traveled

Are you beginning to suspect that healing may lie beyond the doctor's office? Are you willing to look there? Then you're looking down the path back to health.

Do you want to travel this path? Are you sure? Are you really, really sure? Because it won't be easy. If you decide to take responsibility for your health—to take it away from your doctor and reclaim it for yourself —you may be putting yourself on a difficult and scary path—a path with unfamiliar scenery that gives you a hundred reasons to turn back.

This path provides no guarantees. It has no definite end. It sometimes seems to go on and on, and after years of walking it, you may be discouraged to discover you're still not at your destination of full health. Yes, you'll see that you're making progress, but it may be in fits and starts and fraught with detours and roadblocks and sudden setbacks. Your doctor may dump you. Your friends might ridicule you. Your family may accuse you of killing yourself. And you'll have to pay for many treatments out of your own pocket, because most insurance companies won't. Plus, you may have to give up a lot—perhaps your favorite foods or activities, or your habitual patterns of thought and emotion.

But if you've been given a death sentence, you may live anyway. That's the trade-off. Even though you've been told your illness is incurable, you might become disease-free. That's the destination. You won't have to suffer through surgeries or poison your body with toxic drugs. Is it worth it to you?

If so, read on. In this section, we'll look at how the self-healers ran into various stumbling blocks, suffered deep heartaches, and how they kept on.

We'll also see what they did to make the journey quicker and easier—how they hired health-care practitioners to accompany them on the journey, how they did their own research to build their knowledge of their diseases, how they learned to be their own guinea pigs and experiment on themselves.

These are the three interstate freeways on the journey back to health, because they speed it up. If you're anxious to get well, do all three:
• Work with healing professionals.
• Research.
• Experiment.

Now, let's see how the self-healers did it.

A Word of Caution

These stories are *not* meant to outline a treatment protocol for you. If you're a beginning self-healer, you need to do a lot more research before deciding what's best for you.

For example, you'll read about bloodroot used both internally and externally. I would not recommend internal use unless you're an experienced self-healer who is used to working with herbs.

These stories *are* meant to motivate and inspire—to show that people can and do cure themselves of chronic and "incurable" diseases.

They are also meant to provide you with some initial resources to begin your own research. Therefore, resources are listed at the end of each chapter. For quick acces to the Internet resources listed, go to the Resources page of www.tolifeonline.com.

Chapter 40

Linda Koep
and the Long Haul

T he path back to wellness can be fraught with roadblocks, not the least of which are fear and doubt. Are you doing the right thing? Maybe the doctors are right after all. Should you go back? The allopathic illusion tugged at Linda Koep during the first year of her self-healing journey. Three times, medical doctors tried to coax her off the path, using tools ranging from fear to ridicule. Twice they succeeded. But they were only able to divert her for a short period of time. She had begun to think for herself, to trust her ability to observe what is true. With that new skill, she kept looking for a way out of her illnesses.

The last we heard of Linda, she was on her way to a chiropractor's office and had pulled off the road to cry, so hopeless was she that she'd ever feel normal again. She had been diagnosed with seven diseases, was down to one hundred and twelve pounds, was still blacking out and had been labeled a mental-health case. She thought one more health practitioner would not help. But the chiropractor gave her hope, pulling together a team of health professionals—a Chinese medicine practioner, a massage therapist, a holistic dentist, a physical therapist and MDs at an allergy clinic.

Linda stopped taking psychoactive drugs that day. She cancelled her next series of appointments with the psychiatrist. "The doctor called a few weeks later and said he was very concerned that I had cancelled, because I was 'very ill,' and he believed I would not get well without drugs. He said he was hoping I was still taking them," Linda recalls. "It threw this little bit of doubt into my thinking. But it lasted for a second only. I said I'd be in touch with him if and when I needed him, but at this point, I was doing something else."

Linda was becoming empowered. She was beginning to take responsibility for her health. Instead of going back to the psychiatrist, she began to work on her health issues with the new group of practitioners.

"It seemed like I was seeing someone almost every day. I got so involved in my care, it really helped me to gain confidence," Linda recalls. And she began feeling better, too. "I noticed a slight improvement. There was improvement because I now had hope."

But hope alone doesn't cure, and Linda had a very long way to go.

At the allergy clinic, Linda underwent numerous tests. "They were MDs but pretty progressive. Everyone was suspecting that with the breakdown of my body systems, I had become allergic to everything," Linda recalls. "I was diagnosed with environmental illness. I was pretty much sensitive to everything they tested me for, including all food. They did double-blind testing, so even the nurse didn't know what I was being tested on. With the wheat, they had to give me oxygen; with the rice, I'd fall asleep." The doctors prescribed nystatin, an anti-fungal that kills candida yeast in the body. As the yeast cells die, they release powerful toxins that create extreme fatigue, nausea and other symptoms.

"They mentioned candida. But they didn't prepare me for the die-off," Linda says. "With the die-off, I went backwards. I was so thin, I couldn't afford to feel worse, and I did. I started to lose more weight. My bowel transit time was about an hour. I had this toxic, gnawing, aching feeling from my mouth all the way through my entire body."

The new symptoms Linda felt from the die-off were a clue pointing her in the right direction. She had considered candida as a possible culprit for her illness once before.

"My husband had driven me to my last appointment with the psychiatrist, and I had him drop me at the library on the way home. I sat on the floor, because I was too dizzy to sit in a chair. Candida came up in my research that day," Linda recalls. "I was starting to get clued in a bit but had no idea where to go for a diagnosis. At some point, when I mentioned candida to a family practice doctor, she laughed at me and said, 'Honey, only people with AIDS and and cancer get that. That's not it.' So I put it out of my mind." Back then, Linda was still in the habit of trusting the experts.

When the chiropractor put together Linda's health-care team, one on the list was a holistic dentist. He removed a root canal, and Linda began feeling better. But most important to her recovery was a bit of information the dentist gave her. At the end of the first appointment, he handed Linda a piece of paper with a woman's name and phone number.

The woman told Linda about how she recovered from systemic candida infection—also called candidiasis—using a program from Attogram Corporation in Canada. It consisted of ingesting caprylic acid with bentonite clay and psyllium powder while avoiding all sugar and products containing yeast. Linda decided to try it.

"I started the program feeling sorry for myself, because it was just one more thing, but within a couple days, I realized it was helping," Linda recalls.

Because her digestion was so poor, the allergy clinic had recommended she eat one or two tablespoons of food every twenty minutes. "With every tablespoon, I'd pray that something would stick, because I was withering away." On the Attogram program, her digestion improved, starting the healing process.

When she reported her progress at the allergy clinic, the allopaths tried to pull her off her newfound path.

"It's a very progressive clinic at a teaching hospital, but they're still MDs, and this was a program they didn't know about. They didn't want to take the time to familiarize themselves with it," Linda recalls. "I tried to explain that I felt so toxic with the nystatin. They felt the Attogram program was unproven and planted doubt about its long-term effectiveness. And I really wanted to get well. So I went back to the nystatin instead of Attogram for about a week, and I felt myself sliding backwards again."

Once again, Linda had to make a choice. Trust the doctors or trust her own experience? "I decided that I had to follow my own instincts, and I quit going to the allergy clinic," she said. Instead, she resumed the Attogram program and continued with her chiropractor, using muscle testing to find out which supplements her body needed.

"It was kind of like peeling the layers of an onion," Linda says. "I had many ups and downs, and throughout the roller-coaster ride, I always wondered if I was on the right track, because it took so long."

She felt better and better, and within three years had returned to her normal, healthy self.

"Everything in my life was so 'Wow!' I was so amazed at the journey, and I was so grateful to have my life back. I no longer took things for granted, and even the small things seemed incredible."

Linda decided to try to help others and became a distributor for Attogram. But she has learned from her healing journey that neither Attogram nor any one other treatment can be considered a silver-bullet cure.

"You have to hit it from all sides. There is no magic pill," Linda says. "It took diet, exercise, bodywork, nutritional support, dental work, a positive attitude, hope and faith. Don't give up hope. That's the most important thing."

Candidiasis—What Is It?

Candida albicans is a yeast that occurs naturally in the digestive tract. It becomes the disease candidiasis when it changes its structure to the fungal form and grows out of control, infecting other areas of the body.

For more information about candidiasis, its causes and its cures, check these books and Web sites:

- *Conquering Yeast Infections: The Non-Drug Solution for Men and Women*, by S. Colet Lahoz, RN. The author operates the East West Clinic in Minnesota.
- www.wholeapproach.com (Linda's company).
- www.cdc.gov/ncidod/dbmd/diseaseinfo/candidiasis_t.htm (the Center for Disease Control's candidiasis page).

The Candidiasis Cure

- Avoid all sugar, alcohol and products containing yeast. These feed the fungus.
- Mix Caprol (which contains caprylic acid), liquid bentonite clay and psyllium powder in water or orange juice and drink it two or three times a day. The Caprol contains a fungicide extracted from coconut oil. An alternative to Caprol is grapefruit seed extract, another potent anti-fungal. The bentonite clay is volcanic ash that absorbs toxins and helps the body eliminate them via the feces. The powdered psyllium husks quickly become gel-like when liquid is added, and the powdered seeds make the gel rough, so it moves like a sponge through the intestinal tract, scraping the colon clean while brushing it with the anti-fungal agent.
- Take supplements of "friendly bacteria" such as Lactobacillus acidophilus, which help keep the intestinal flora in balance.
- Take supplements of soil-based organisms, such as Bacillus subtillis. They engulf the fungi and dislodge hardened wastes stuck to the intestinal wall. Humans used to ingest these when they ate mostly farm-fresh food. But agricultural chemicals have virtually eliminated these beneficial organisms from our diets.

Chapter 41

Tricia Bies and the High Cost of Healing

You'll recall Tricia Bies, the woman whose tumor plopped out onto the floor. Her story shows that if you dare to treat yourself, you'll have to pay for it, both financially and emotionally.

Let's go back to the day Tricia's doctor recommended a radical mastectomy for her cancer, infiltrating ductile carcinoma. Two days after that recommendation, she made the decision not to do it. She decided to not even have a lumpectomy. Then she called her brother—the one who twenty-seven years ago was supposed to die as a result of his embryonic cell carcinoma.

"He put me on a diet that he's been on his whole life. He's been in the nutritional field ever since he cured his cancer. He believes cancer grows in an acidic environment, so if you can get your body in an alkaline state, you can be cancer free."

So Tricia began the diet, which eliminates dairy, sugar, caffeine, wheat, meat and salt. She also began detoxifying her body with a juice fast one day every week, followed by a colonic irrigation (a procedure that cleans the entire length of the colon). She began talking to women who'd had breast cancer, and she began reading books about cancer. A mammogram three months later showed the tumors had not increased in size, so Tricia figured she was on the right track.

Then she ran into an acquaintance in the grocery store—a woman who also had cancer and who told Tricia about a compound that would bring the tumor to the surface and expel it through the skin.

"I thought, 'Yeah, right.' But my brother had heard of it and that it works, but it's hard to get a hold of. This lady gave it to me in a small container. It looks like red mud."

Because it was Tricia's first foray into natural medicine, she did not know that the red mud was simply bloodroot—the root of a weed that grows in the northeastern United States and has been used by Native Americans for centuries to get rid of skin cancers. She didn't know anything about it, just that it had cured someone else's cancer.

"For the first two weeks, you put this red mud in a capsule and take it orally. At the end of that, you put it on topically. It makes the tumor go into a ball, draws ganglions to the surface. That caused pain down to my elbow, down my side and up my neck. I didn't sleep for two weeks. At the end of the two weeks, these tumors were two hard balls at the surface; they looked like you could slit the skin and pull them out. By now, the pain was so bad I couldn't use my left arm. There were nights when I would lay on the couch and just weep."

In spite of the pain, Tricia dared not go to the doctor. Though frightened by what was happening, she continued following the protocol outlined by the woman who gave her the red mud.

That's one of the ways the allopathic medical system penalizes people for treating themselves. It makes no information about alternative cures available, so you sometimes have to work without knowledge, and that can be frightening, especially when you're in pain.

"I put this substance on the surface for three days. Now you have a dried up poultice with gauze dried onto your skin. I thought, if they take me to the hospital, they'll put me in the loony bin. It's as if I have some disease from Africa. It was inflamed and red up to my neck. After a few days, I could see it was starting to come away from the skin, like a cake comes away from a pan. We called it the booby hatch." Tricia explains the humorous term: "If you don't laugh some of the time, you cry all the time."

When the tumor plopped onto the floor like a dead oyster, Tricia was shocked speechless. Where the tumor had been, a bloody crater remained.

"I put a colander over it. I didn't dare go to the doctor. As soon as I could touch it, I put Neosporin™ over it. The whole thing was about six weeks from the time I put the red mud on until it healed enough to put clothes over it."

When Tricia could finally touch the wound, she felt a lump underneath.

"I was devastated. I thought, 'If it's going to come out in layers, I can't go through this again."

She finally went to a doctor. He told her that the tumor came through the skin on its own, not because of the bloodroot. The doctor not only discounted the bloodroot as possibly having an impact on her tumor, he let her know there was a penalty for taking matters into her own hands.

"I said, 'We have the tumor at home in the freezer.' But he said he didn't want to see it, because it's been contaminated. I really didn't want to see him again. He said, 'Because you've done this thing, there's nothing I can sew to that.'" In other words, a lumpectomy was no longer an option. At the same time, he expressed surprise that the second tumor was not connected to her chest tissues. "He said, 'I'm just so amazed it's so loose.'" (An herbalist, knowing that bloodroot causes cancer cells to collect together in a ball, then separate from non-cancerous tissue, would not have been amazed.)

Tricia allowed an operation, and when she returned for an examination, the same doctor was again surprised by her condition. "He said, 'Maybe you should keep doing what you're doing. You have no cancer in your body,'" Tricia recalls. "Talk about good news. We went dancing out of there."

But a little less than a year later, Tricia felt a hard ball below her rib cage. "My husband felt it and went white. I went whiter."

A CAT scan showed four tumors, one the size of a racquetball, three the size of golf balls. They were in her liver and malignant. The breast cancer had metastasized.

"Liver cancer is a biggie. I've heard it's the one you never get rid of. The news knocked us on our heels, but it didn't knock us out. Glenn (Tricia's husband) said, 'We can do this, too.' When I had breast cancer, I asked Glenn, 'How can we get through this?' Glenn had said, 'The same way you eat an elephant: one bite at a time.'"

Tricia again called her brother. He had remained cancer-free for nearly three decades thanks to diet, but he initially eliminated his cancer by taking vitamin B17, also known as laetrile. Laetrile is unavailable in the United States, so people who want to use it must go to Mexico. Mexican laetrile clinics typically cost about one thousand dollars per day. Most are run by MDs who use modern, high-tech medical devices combined with a holistic approach. But medical insurance doesn't cover these clinics, in spite of the fact that their success rates are high.

That's another way monopoly medicine punishes medical rebels; it pays only for its treatments.

If Tricia wanted to follow her brother's example and live, she'd have to pay for it out of pocket. She and her husband reasoned that people spend twenty-thousand dollars for a car, so why not spend that much for a life? They borrowed money from Tricia's two brothers and went to Mexico.

The clinic's protocol included laetrile, shark cartilage, megadoses of vitamins C and B, magnesium, potassium, a hormone blocker and a chelating agent called EDTA. Tricia had a coffee enema every other day and a colonic irrigation each week. The food was vegetarian and organic.

After one week, Tricia woke up laying on her right side—something she hadn't done in weeks, because it hurt due to the lumps in her liver. She stayed for seventeen days of treatment, and she returned to the United States in May 2001 with an I.V. bag and three-thousand-dollars-worth of supplements, shark cartilage and liquid laetrile—enough to last three months.

Two months later, a test showed a dramatic decrease in tumor size. Tricia was elated. During the next doctor's visit, the oncologist said Tricia's liver was irritated and suggested she take chemotherapy. "He said, 'If you don't do it for yourself, do it for your children,'" Tricia recalls. "I started crying. It's no wonder people succumb to that."

She had again experienced a way in which the medical monopoly castigates medical rebels—with guilt. But Tricia didn't cave in. She had learned about the need for a strong immune system to fight her cancer. And she didn't want to take chemicals that would harm that immune system.

"I hear people say, 'The doctor said I needed it; I had no choice.' But they do have a choice," she says.

For the next six months, Tricia's tumors kept shrinking. She was still using laetrile—injecting it through a catheter—and receiving no help from her doctors for her self-treatment. When she started bleeding through the catheter, she became frightened. She took the cap off the end of the catheter and saw a large blood clot. "I was fortunate to find a surgeon willing to remove the old catheter and replace it. However, when I asked him what kind of dressing I should put on this new catheter, he said, 'I don't really care how you dress it.'"

Again, monopoly medicine was withdrawing its support after begrudgingly helping her with the catheter.

"It isn't all that easy being in charge of and taking responsibility for my own health care sometimes. I can see why people want to leave all the decisions up to the doctors and make them responsible if it works or not. A person who uses alternative treatments needs to expect little, if any, support from the traditional medical arena," Tricia wrote in an e-mail.

But there finally came a time when Tricia needed that support. The tumors in her liver began growing again. They were again causing pain.

"Four doctors said if you don't get those tumors smaller, you will die," Tricia said. "I looked at my husband and said, 'I have no fight left.'"

Every day she continued distilling water, juicing carrots, doing shark cartilage enemas, injecting laetrile and sticking to a strict diet. So much effort for so long, and she still had tumors. She needed to shrink the tumors. Tricia needed help from the doctors for awhile.

"I can see why people go in and say to the doctor, 'Do your thing,'" she says.

She traveled to Mayo Clinic, but doctors said there was nothing more they could do. "It was very profound to sit at Mayo Clinic, the mecca of medical science, and hear them say, 'We can't help you,'" Tricia recalls. She was devastated and cried in sorrow.

Then she and her husband left the clinic and went shopping for food for a family party. They were going to be staying at a friend's cabin for a few days, and their children were going to join them. "How many people are handed a death sentence, then they plan a party?" Tricia asks. "I did have some fight left."

Sunday morning at the cabin, the family held its own private church service and talked about their feelings regarding Tricia's cancer. "I said my fear was that the kids would get bitter and not deal with it in a healthy way," Tricia recalls. "Then this feeling of peace came over me." She felt that somehow, things would work out.

She went home and decided to let the doctors give her chemotherapy. Nearly three years after telling herself she'd never take chemotherapy, she chose to do it. But it is a type of chemotherapy as close to natural medicine as allopathy gets. Just prior to publication of this book, Tricia's doctor was treating her with the drug Taxol™—developed from an extract of the Pacific Yew tree—while she continued to treat herself with laetrile and a modified diet. She chose to combine alternative and allopathic methods to give the tumors a double whammy.

She also chose to postpone the chemotherapy a few days so that she could take a fermented soy product that keeps blood counts high during chemotherapy. A blood test after her first round of Taxol showed a normal white count, which is abnormal for chemo patients.

"The doctors are astounded I don't have cancer in other organs. I'm as fit as a fiddle," Tricia said in March 2002, a week before the second of three Taxol infusions. "One doctor, my oncologist, said he and the other doctors talk about their cases, and they're all amazed I'm still alive."

And she's using every treatment at her disposal to stay that way.

For More Information

Here's where you can find out more about some of the treatments Tricia used:

- *Tijuana Clinics,* by Sally Wolper. This reference book describes all the hospitals and medical centers in Tijuana, Mexico, that offer alternative therapies for various diseases, including cancer. It also describes how the therapies work. Those therapies include laetrile, Gerson therapy, metabolic therapy, live cell therapy, chelation and oxygen therapy.

- *Alkalize or Die,* by Theodore A. Baroody. This book explains how disease thrives in an acidic body and what you can do to keep your body alkaline.

- *Dr. Jensen's Guide to Better Bowel Care: A Complete Program for Tissue Cleansing Through Bowel Management,* by Bernard Jensen. This book includes information on how to do colonic irrigation at home.

- *The Story of Taxol: Nature and Politics in the Pursuit of an Anti-Cancer Drug,* by Jordan Goodman and Vivien Walsh. This book outlines how Taxol, extracted from the bark of the Pacific yew tree, became an important anti-tumor agent in allopathy's cancer-fighting arsenal.

Black Salve and Healing Salve

When Tricia treated her tumors with bloodroot salve, she didn't know what it was. Neither did she know how to treat the wound left after the "red mud" extracted the tumor. Below are recipes and treatment protocols for bloodroot paste, also known as black salve, and a healing salve for after-care. Black salve is perhaps the most intense and painful cancer salve. The recipe is included here, not because it's the best choice, but because it's what Tricia Bies used. For a look at all the cancer salves, including detailed descriptions of use, read *Cancer Salves: A Botanical Approach to Treatment,* by Ingrid Naiman.

Black Salve Recipe

40 % Bloodroot (powdered)
50 % Zinc chloride
10 % White flour

Mix ingredients together with distilled water. Under low heat, stir until ingredients dissolve, adding more flour as necessary to thicken to consistency of toothpaste.

Healing Salve Recipe

1 pint linseed oil
1/2 ounce lavender oil
2 cakes of white beeswax (approx. 3 ounces
   at the consistency of Vaseline)
1 piece of rosin

Heat the linseed oil, beeswax and rosin until all are dissolved. Remove from the heat and cool somewhat before adding lavender oil.

Instructions for use

Apply the black salve to the tumor. Over a period of one to three days, it will dry, then it should fall off along with the tumor. Then apply the healing salve every day for at least five days.

Alternate method

Apply the black salve to the tumor for twenty-four hours. Remove it and apply the healing salve for the next five days, changing the bandage every day. Clean the area with hydrogen peroxide if needed. Apply the black salve again for twenty-four hours, then use the healing salve each day until the tumor comes off. The skin underneath should be pink and healed.

Chapter 42

Sarah Clemente
and Being Different

When you use natural rather than chemical means to treat yourself, you'll face ridicule, both subtle and outright. People fear what they don't know, and one way to handle that fear is to discount the unknown or make fun of it. Your doctor may tell you you're being foolish. Family members may try to talk you out of it. Friends may make fun of you. If you're a teenager, it's especially difficult to face.

When Sarah Clemente chose a different treatment for diabetes at age twelve, the only thing she did that differed from her peers was to eat all her food uncooked. Her classmates understood insulin shots; that's something the doctor says you have to do. But this food was raw—not fried chicken and sandwiches and candy bars, but alfalfa sprouts and sun-dried olives and bizarre fruits that her classmates had never seen. Some of Sarah's classmates poked fun. It hurt. But Sarah stuck with it, because she no longer had to give herself daily insulin shots.

Now she looks at the other kids' food and finds it unappealing. "I wonder how people can eat that stuff," she says of the typical American diet. "I would never go back to the other way of eating. This diet makes me feel so much better."

It wasn't just Sarah's classmates who didn't want her to be different; it was her doctors, too. "They don't run into people doing what we are doing," says Sarah's mother, Sue. "They keep trying to put her back on insulin. This is what the doctors know."

But Sue knew of something different. As a teenager, Sue had intestinal problems and went to doctors for help. She, too, had been indoctrinated in the belief that when you're ill, you go to the doctor, period. But the doctors were not able to help her completely heal. So when Sue became an adult, she decided to do her own research. She went to the library for books and went to health food stores to ask questions.

"My grandma died of colon cancer when I was about ten. I never saw her smile. She was always sick. She was in pain, and I didn't want to die that way. The doctors couldn't help me, but I knew there had to be an answer someplace."

So she researched and learned about diet and nutrition. She noticed she felt better when she ate certain foods and avoided others. So she modified her nutritional intake. She began drinking wheatgrass juice and growing her own sunflower and buckwheat sprouts. She stopped consuming white flour, sugar, dairy food, chocolate and meats.

Then she heard about a healing clinic called Hippocrates Health Institute and wanted to go. This Florida healing center teaches people to boost their immune systems through diet, exercise and positive attitude. Sue had not gone, because she didn't think she could afford the fee for a three-week visit. But when her daughter's future was on the line, she found a way. When Sarah got sick, Sue accompanied her to Hippocrates to learn how to live on a living foods diet.

After being diagnosed, Sarah had gained twenty-five pounds in several weeks—a situation that is not unusual for people who begin taking insulin. "She was an emotional wreck every day by late afternoon," Sue recalls. "Her blood sugar when first diagnosed was at 430."

Within the first three days at Hippocrates, Sarah was in the normal zone for blood sugar: 80 and 120. "After three weeks at Hippocrates, she was a whole different person," Sarah says. "We were lowering the insulin dosage quickly—a unit or two a day. Her emotions were even. She was beginning to lose the extra weight."

Now, Sarah keeps insulin handy just in case she needs it, but she says she goes for months without it. To begin controlling her diabetes, she just had to eat raw foods and exercise vigorously.

Sue's years of research and experimentation paid off, both for herself and for her daughter.

"The one who gets the success is the one who works at it the most and longest," Sue says. "Edison tried and tried before he came up with the light bulb. So keep reading. Keep asking questions. And don't give up."

Especially don't give up when family, friends and medical professionals ridicule your choices, Sue says. They're not the ones who have the disease.

Clinics for Diabetics Seeking Natural Cures

- The Hippocrates Institute in West Palm Beach, Florida, works from the premise that an enzyme-rich diet, non-invasive therapies and positive thinking are the most important elements for full health. It may be reached at 1443 Palmdale Court, West Palm Beach, FL, 33411.

    Phone: 1-561-471-8876;
    E-mail: info@hippocratesinst.com;
    Web site: www.hippocratesinst.com
- The Weimar Institute works from the premise that diabetes is a lifestyle disease. It may be reached at P.O. Box 486, Weimar, CA, 95736.

    Phone: 1-800-525-9192;
    E-mail: communications@weimar.org;
    Web site: www.weimar.org

Chapter 43

Madhuri Cawley and the Illness Onion

With degrees, training and work experience in several disciplines, including psychology, allopathic medicine and holistic medicine, Madhuri Cawley was better equipped than most to diagnose and cure what she called "brain fog." Still, it took her a dozen years to recover from a complicated web of related symptoms.

Her story illustrates four of the classic features of the journey from chronic illness to health:

- You're in it for the long haul and are likely to suffer setbacks.
- You'll have to deal with a host of health-related issues. Like peeling the layers of an onion, resolving one health problem often uncovers another.
- Working with one or more health care practitioners can hasten your recovery.
- You may have to go beyond their advice and be your own guinea pig.

Madhuri was attending pre-medical school when she noticed that she was frequently irritable and couldn't concentrate. She decided to get professional opinions—not one, but six. And she chose to get those opinions from health-care practitioners who had the knowledge to deal with systemic illness. So she went to three holistic doctors and three chiropractors.

"If I had gone to (allopathic) MDs, I would've been put on antidepressants and medicines for pain, because they wouldn't believe a person that young could have brain fog. To them, it wouldn't exist," Madhuri says. Her combined background in natural and allopathic medicine gave her the conviction that it was worth paying out of pocket for unconventional treatments. She wanted something that would cure her condition, not anti-depressants and painkillers to mask it.

One holistic MD diagnosed systemic candida, a yeast infection. He suggested Madhuri take digestive enzymes and improve her nutrition. He also prescribed black-walnut-hull extract for bringing the candida back in balance.

Since Madhuri could prescribe medication, she filled a prescription for nystatin—a powerful anti-fungal. She also took caprylic acid as a fungus fighter. She decided to take milk thistle seed to support her liver, because candida produces powerful toxins, and it's the liver's job to clean them out of the body.

With the ability to get chemical drugs and knowledge of natural substances, she was perfectly suited to try every possible substance that might contribute to a cure.

"I can't even guess how many different things I tried. I was guinea pigging myself," she said. She gave each substance or method one to three months before trying the next. Some improved her symptoms; some made her feel worse—a result of the toxicity that ensues when the yeast organisms die off quickly.

She went to one chiropractor who adjusted her jaw and cranium. Another used neuro-emotional techniques. Another said she should have her silver fillings removed from her teeth.

"That was the worst thing anyone could have told me, because I was so fearful of dental work," Madhuri recalls. She suffered for two more years before deciding to take that route. "Finally, I bit the bullet. It was 1987. By then, I had had to quit school, and my marriage was suffering, because I was flipped out from my toxicity, and I had had systemic candida for years." She finally made the appointment and had thirteen large, mercury-amalgam fillings taken out of her teeth.

"It was hell," she says. "But the day after my last filling was removed, I felt eighty percent better. The fog lifted. I could concentrate, think, talk, make sentences. My mind returned."

Madhuri believes that all the other methods and substances she tried were effective but not the full solution. "They all worked to a certain extent, but not until my amalgams were removed did I realize the benefit of it all. This is what got me ill; this is what was keeping me ill," she says. "Mercury-amalgam poisoning is a precursor to yeast and can lead to debilitating illnesses like herpes and then cancer."

Over the next several years, she worked to clean the toxins out of her blood and tissues using chlorophyll, garlic and a chelating agent called DMSA.

One symptom—fatigue—started coming back, and by 1994, Madhuri had so little energy that she could barely work. Tests showed she had low thyroid and poorly functioning adrenal glands. She studied the glandular system and began taking natural hydrocortisone and DHEA for the adrenals and natural whole thyroid. Within a week, she could function again.

But her journey back to health still was not over. The toxins had caused yeast overgrowth; bringing it back into balance was the top layer of Madhuri's illness onion. Once that layer was gone, it revealed the next: The toxins had also caused some of her glands to function poorly. Madhuri gained the knowledge to repair the glandular damage. Still, she was not done. The toxins and poor nutrition also had worn away the membrane that covers the nerve cells, called the myelin sheath. That, too, had to be repaired.

For many months, Madhuri had occasionally experienced the classic symptoms of multiple sclerosis—a disease caused by disintegration of the myelin sheath. So she did biochemical and fatty acid analyses of her red cell membranes. She discovered a depletion of the fatty acids that make up the myelin sheath. She also discovered that her cell membranes were rigid, making it difficult for the cells to absorb the things they need and expel wastes.

Madhuri took a protein supplement to repair the myelin sheath and took minerals that increase the permeability of the cells in the intestines.

MDs are taught in medical school that MS is incurable. But Madhuri's MS symptoms have never returned.

Now, she has a busy medical consultation practice specializing in natural hormone therapy. Patients around the country come to her to get their glands back in balance. And now, she's the one recommending that people have their amalgam fillings taken out.

Deadly Dental Work?

Whether dental amalgam fillings and root canals cause health problems is now a hotly debated subject.

Holistic dentist and author Hal Huggins says that in the case of root canals, the bacteria trapped in the dead tooth mutate in order to live without oxygen, and in that mutation, they produce a strong toxin that then leeches into the body.

In the case of mercury-amalgam fillings, it is known that mercury leaks from fillings and that mercury poisoning can cause anxiety, headache and fatigue. But dentists who use amalgam believe the amount released is too little to cause illness. The position of the American Dental Association is that no controlled studies have been done to prove adverse health effects from either amalgam fillings or root canals.

Numerous books and Web sites explain theories of how dental work —specifically amalgam fillings and root canals—may cause health problems. Books and Web sites with pertinent information include:

- *Whole-Body Dentistry: Discover The Missing Piece To Better Health,* by Mark A. Breiner, DDS, and Robert C. Atkins, MD. The authors say that many dentists are losing their licenses for removing amalgam fillings, because the American Dental Association is trying to protect its position that amalgam is safe.
- *Uninformed Consent: The Hidden Dangers in Dental Care*, by Hal A. Huggins, DDS, Thomas E. Levy, MD, and James L. Merrill. The authors say metal toxins cause a wide range of diseases, including multiple sclerosis, Alzheimer's disease, Parkinson's disease, chronic fatigue syndrome and leukemia.

- *Root Canal Cover-Up*, by George Meinig, DDS. The author, one of the founders of the American Association of Endodontists, learned of the health hazards of root canals after reading the work of Dr. Weston Price, the American Dental Association's first director of research.
- www.yourhealthbase.com/amalgams.html (summaries of recent scientific studies on amalgam fillings).
- www.citizens.org/AlternativeMedicine/CDCP/dental.htm (the Web site of Consumers for Dental Choice).

Chapter 44

Jacquie Compton and the Medical Magnet

You'll recall Jacquie Compton—the woman who heard her death sentence when the doctor looked away from her and addressed her husband instead; the woman who, after five surgeries, was supposed to die within two years from cancer.

Knowing that she was going to lose her life allowed Jacquie to consider every option. No matter what she did, she had nothing more to lose. She already had lost everything. So why not try non-medical alternatives?

A neighbor gave Jacquie some nutritional information, and she decided to try a few of the things she read about. She stopped eating meat and sugar. She stopped eating food that had been treated with pesticides, herbicides and chemical fertilizers. She dug up her back yard, put in a garden and started raising chickens so that she had access to organic foods. Within six months of keeping chemicals out of her food, she felt better. She was no longer seventy-two pounds and barely able to function. Life was returning.

Jacquie tried various things suggested by a woman at the local health food store; she doesn't remember exactly what. The woman belonged to a small church "where they read the Bible and believed it was true, and they all seemed intelligent." So Jacquie began reading scripture. She also paid attention to her negative patterns of thought and worked to break those patterns.

"I had changed my mind and body, and now I also knew I had a spiritual connection that I didn't have before," Jacquie recalls. "I now had a contentment, a peacefulness throughout my being. Then, even though

205

there were bouts of extreme vomiting and weakness, they became less frequent, shorter in duration and less confining."

Jacquie had become a convert, not only spiritually, but also health-wise. She thought about natural versus manmade substances, and through a process of logical reasoning, she realized that chemical drugs and chemically treated foods cannot lead to healing.

"If you believe and understand that you are an organic, living structure, it stands to reason that that structure can only use living, organically structured things to add to its life source, because even though man and science can create things in the laboratory, they have yet failed to create life. They can imitate it, they can counterfeit it, but they can't create it," she says.

To explain how the body reacts to chemicals, she asks you to imagine holding a small child and looking into a mirror. "If you say to the child, 'Give me a kiss,' the baby does not lean forward and kiss that mirror, it turns its head to kiss you. That baby realizes what's in the mirror is not the real thing," Jacquie says. "We can give our body imitation food and prescription drugs, but our body in its wisdom approaches it and says, "Oops! Not real, not real, not real."

So Jacquie stopped putting non-natural things in her body. As time went on, she just kept feeling better and better. There was no magic bullet, no sudden healing, no dramatic miracle, just a slow and steady improvement.

Eventually, she was cancer free.

"I attribute it to cleaning up my diet, properly nourishing my body, getting rid of negative ways of acting and thinking, and my spiritual transformation," Jacquie says. "I didn't go to a doctor for years. I was living life. It made sense to me: If I wasn't dead, I must be alive."

For a quarter century, Jacquie just lived. But life in North America does not lend itself to health. Jacquie began allowing herself to sometimes eat the typical grocery store and restaurant food. Eating organic food is not a mainstream thing to do, so it takes time and effort. She also allowed herself to drink Diet Coke.

Jacquie had taken a job as a senior administrator in an international law firm, even though she knew it was not a good environment for her. But the mainstream American value is to put up with a less-than-ideal work situation in exchange for good pay. So she stayed.

"I got sick again because I lost my way," Jacquie says. "If you hike, you know that if you take one step off the path, it's easy to get back on. But if you keep walking away from the path, you can't find your way back."

Now, with one foot back in the mainstream world, it didn't take long for Jacquie to get sidetracked from the natural-healing path. Jacquie's law firm had three female executives, and they decided to organize a walkathon for breast cancer awareness.

"We decided to go through the mammogram process to lead the way," Jacquie recalls. "That's how subtly you get drawn back into the medical world."

The next time she started feeling ill, she was still off the natural-healing path, so she went to the doctor. A friend suggested some herbs, and she took them, but she also took prescription drugs and kept her doctor appointments. "They'd do the poke-me-pull-me-suck-the-blood thing, then they'd say, 'Okay, let's try this drug, and they'd discontinue the old one,'" Jacquie says. "This bag of discontinued medicines kept getting bigger, and I knew I wasn't getting well."

Her anxiety grew, and she went to a psychologist. It was a quirky twist of fate at the psychologist's office that returned Jacquie to the healing path.

As Jacquie tells it, "They psychologist said, 'Ask your doctor for a juice bar; it will help the anxiety.' So my mind is scrambling to figure this out. I know juices are important, but how will it help with this?" Later, Jacquie saw a magazine ad for an anti-anxiety drug pronounced "boosbar" and realized this is what the psychologist was talking about.

It made her mad. And that was her turning point—the moment when she decided to stop wandering through the allopathic world and get back to her healing path. "It said it was for anxiety that is not reality based. I thought, how dare you? I felt totally discounted as a person, just like when the doctor spoke to my husband instead of me. I thought, I'm not going to put any more pills in that plastic bag. It's that moment of honesty when you sit down and take a look at who you are and what you're doing and how you want to live."

Jacquie decided to stay with natural food and medicine only. She is well again. As a reminder, she keeps that plastic bag full of prescription medicines that didn't work.

Killer Cuisine

After five operations and a death sentence, Jacquie Compton cured her cancer through attitude and spiritual practice and by eliminating chemicals from her food.

The National Academy of Sciences issued a report in 1987 that predicted that pesticides alone would cause more than one million cancer cases in the United States over the next seventy years. Yet agricultural chemicals—pesticides, herbicides and fertilizers—exist in almost every food item pulled off a grocery story shelf.

Some grocery stores advertise produce with "no detectible pesticide residue," but these are not necessarily safe. The U.S. General Accounting Office estimates that about half of all pesticides cannot be detected by FDA laboratories. The only way to avoid agricultural chemicals in food is to grow your own or buy only those foods labeled organic.

Chapter 45

Annie Wilkin and the Search for a Healer

When you are very ill, it helps to have a health-practitioner partner. But you may have to try out various healing professionals before you find one who has the skills you need, just like you may have to try out various healing substances before you find the one that works.

For Annie Wilkin, health practitioner number eleven was an acupuncturist. This was the advice he gave her one day when she came to his office during one of her near-blackout episodes: "Next time this happens, please go to the emergency room instead of coming here."

But Annie had given up on doctors and hospitals. Her episodes had brought her to emergency rooms twice. At one, the doctor said she was suffering a bout of gastroenteritis. At another, she was diagnosed with an allergic reaction to mosquito bites. A family practice physician had done a battery of tests and concluded that Annie had typhoid fever. Another said it was allergies indeed, but to ants, not mosquitoes.

All four of these MDs announced their diagnoses with complete confidence. Not one prefaced it with, "I'm not sure, but you may be suffering from..." They seemed to know what was wrong. Yet none of their treatments worked.

MDs are not trained to diagnose many of today's common chronic ailments, particularly those caused by parasites or environmental chemicals—or, in Annie's case, a combination of both. Thus, they not only fail to cure, they worsen this situation by treating for illnesses that aren't there, adding chemical drugs to bodies already struggling to cope with a chemical overload.

Because their treatments didn't work, and because all four diagnosed different ailments, Annie had to conclude that medical doctors were not competent to help her. They prescribed drugs to treat ailments she didn't have, and the drugs caused additional damage to her body. She began to joke that the initials MD stand for "More Damage."

She began searching elsewhere for help. Before she went to the acupuncturist, she had already tried a homeopathist, two chiropractors, a psychic surgeon from the Philippines and two energy healers. They were exactly the opposite of the MDs. The MDs said they knew what was wrong, but none of their treatments helped. The alternative practitioners said they did not know what was wrong, but their treatments did improve her health. After a year of alternative treatments, however, Annie was still having episodes in which her throat began swelling shut and she began losing consciousness.

No one had told her that the patient can do her own medical research. That idea is foreign to the American way of thinking, so it never crossed her mind. So she kept going from practitioner to practitioner, hoping one would finally figure out what was wrong. Practitioner number twelve was a naturopathic doctor.

"I specialize in worms and germs," the naturopath told Annie. This healing professional had lost her kidneys to pesticide poisoning, so she was particularly knowledgeable about how chemicals impact the body. Like many naturopaths, she held to the credo, "Good health begins and ends in the colon," so she was also knowledgeable about intestinal parasites. She did not pretend to know exactly what was wrong with Annie, but she said she was certain she could help Annie heal. When Annie heard those words, the cloud of fear that had been darkening around her for more than a year began to dissipate.

Sure enough, worms and germs and chemicals were a big part of the problem.

The naturopath treated Annie with herbs, nutrients, bee venom, colonic irrigations and saunas. Most important of all, she shared both her medical knowledge and her personal wisdom. For example, Annie had all the classic symptoms of the first stage of multiple sclerosis. The naturopath showed Annie two medical books that listed nearly identical symptoms for pesticide poisoning and multiple sclerosis. And she taught Annie that it was all right for her to take responsibility for her own health.

And so she was able to take over her own care, doing her own research, experimenting with a wide variety of health products, and slowly getting better and better. Over the next five years, her health literature grew until she had a small library of alternative health books. She used dozens of herbs and nutritional supplements and several bioelectric devices. She went to a Qigong seminar to learn this ancient Chinese healing system. She quit smoking, ate more organic foods and began drinking pure water. She drank colloidal silver and added drops of food-grade hydrogen peroxide to her drinking water. She learned how to keep her body's pH within a healthy range.

To this day, Annie has not been able to give her illness a specific label.

When the doctor labels your symptoms as a specific illness with a fancy name, you're tricked into believing he has all the answers. He doesn't. Naming a disease is not the same as knowing its causes and cures. Annie didn't need a label for her illness, just a cure.

"I told the MDs what was happening in my body. I said I was dying from the inside out. Everything was shutting down," Annie says. "People can tell what's happening in their own bodies if they pay attention. But the doctors wouldn't listen to me."

Annie feels that she is now ninety percent cured. She has decided that the last ten percent of the path back to full health will be accomplished through a raw-food diet, and at the time of publication, she had just switched to a raw foods lifestyle.

Annie has been to an MD only twice since her last misdiagnosis by an emergency room physician. Due to a lump in her breast, she decided to get a mammogram. It showed two "suspicious masses." But Annie felt no fear. She simply took the herbs that she knew—thanks to years of her own research—cure cancer. Six months later, after several calls from the doctor's office urging her to make an appointment for a biopsy, she went in. But she insisted on a follow-up mammogram rather than a biopsy. The lumps were gone. The doctor was surprised, but Annie wasn't.

Parasite Cleansing and Qigong

While Annie's health improved slowly over a period of six years, the "treatments" that propelled her the most quickly down her healing path were parasite cleansing and Qigong.

Annie experimented with several parasite remedies. The most effective was the protocol outlined by naturopath Hulda Clark in her book, *The Cure for All Diseases*. It consists of using black walnut hulls, cloves and wormwood herb to kill all stages of parasites while using a zapper to devitalize them. You can order the three substances in capsule form off of Dr. Clark's Web site, www.huldaclark.com. If you don't like ingesting numerous capsules, several companies make a tincture with all three ingredients combined. You can find it in most health food stores.

A good source for zappers is SOTA Instruments, which may be reached at anybody@sotainstruments.com by e-mail, 1-800-224-0242 by phone, or www.sotainstruments.com on the Internet. The Canadian Health Protection Branch has issued SOTA a license that allows it to sell zappers to people who do not have prescription for them.

Annie learned Qigong at an intensive, one-week seminar. Qigong is a self-healing art of moving meditation that the Chinese have used to cure cancer and immune system disorders. It comes from the root words for "energy" and "skill" and literally means "the skill of attracting vital energy." For more information, go to the Qigong Association of America's Web site at www.qi.org, or read the book *The Way of Qigong: The Art and Science of Chinese Energy Healing*, by Ken Cohen. To learn more about the specific Qigong classes Annie took, go to www.chilel-qigong.com.

Chapter 46

Andrew Yachad and the Power of Research

The course of study that led Andrew Yachad to a career as a nutritional consultant began at age fourteen. It was then that he decided to find out what caused his asthma and what would cure it. The doctor had told him there was no cure, but that an inhaler would control the symptoms.

"The downfall with allopathy is that people are not looking to eradicate the cause. All they want to do is get rid of the symptoms with the least amount of effort from the patient," Andrew says.

Controlling the symptoms with an inhaler wasn't good enough for him. He wanted to play sports. He wanted to be free of the disease. So he went to the library. He learned that asthma is nothing more than irritated mucous membranes, and the biggest irritators are milk and wheat products. He stopped drinking milk and eating bread. It was simple.

"The results were remarkable," Andrew recalls. "Within six months, I was playing soccer and swimming."

He has been on a wheat- and milk-free diet for more than twenty-five years now, and the only thing that sets off an asthmatic reaction is when he inadvertently eats food with chemical flavors or colors or when he's around cigarette smoke.

"Statistics show the number of asthmatic children has skyrocketed, and that's because of our diet," Andrew says. His opinion is based on continued researching of diet and health. Today, he's a nutritional consultant. He says he's mystified that some medical doctors still believe that what people eat does not play a major role in their health. So he encourages those with health problems to do their own research.

"People can be responsible for their own health. They mustn't be duped into thinking they are a bunch of idiots by the doctors, because that furthers dependence on the medical community," he says.

People well educated about how foods work with the body may discover they no longer need doctors, Andrew says. He gives the example of the day he was diagnosed with double pneumonia. The doctor wanted to put Andrew in the hospital. Andrew refused, so the doctor gave him a prescription for antibiotics and said if Andrew's condition did not improve in three days, he had to go to the hospital. Andrew went to the grocery store instead of the drug store. He bought fresh produce—horseradish, red pepper, ginger root and garlic—foods used for centuries throughout the world to kill microbes and clear the lungs. He woke up the next morning with clear lungs.

"That was the defining experience for me that I don't need doctors, except maybe in an extreme emergency," Andrew says.

If he hadn't spent years researching how herbs and foods impact the body, he wouldn't have known what to try. He would have spent time in the hospital on antibiotics. But his prior research had taught him which natural substances would be effective in curing pneumonia. And he had the confidence to give it a try.

There's no excuse to not become educated about your illness, Andrew believes. "I've seen the most unbelievable variety of good books for people who want to get a hold of the information."

Let Food Be Thy Medicine

The father of modern medicine, Hippocrates, said, "Let food be thy medicine and medicine be they food." Some of the self-healers in this book, like Andrew, cured chronic or deadly illnesses by diet change alone. Yet physicians rarely counsel patients on how food harms or heals. The very concept of a dietary connection to health has been taken out of the modern-day Hippocratic Oath—an oath that all medical school students take at graduation.

The original text of the oath begins by outlining the obligations a medical student has toward his teacher and his duty to transmit medical knowledge. The second half contains medical ethics for physicians, the very first of which says, "I will apply dietetic measure for the benefit of the sick according to my ability and judgment." That sentence was deleted from the oath.

No matter what the ailment, the foods taken into the body can hasten or delay its healing.

Chapter 47

Victoria Boutenko and the Value of Anecdotal Evidence

Wh 　hen Victoria Boutenko was told that there was no cure for her arrhythmia, she believed the prognosis. So she didn't go looking for a cure. But when her son, Sergei, lapsed into a diabetic coma, and the doctor said there was no cure for diabetes, she was determined to find an option other than the only one allopathy offered: insulin injections.

She bought Sergei a blood monitor so that he could check his blood sugar level regularly. She made sure he ate no white sugar or white flour. It didn't help. She decided she'd have to become more knowledgeable.

Victoria had spent four years in nursing school in Russia, so she felt qualified to do her own research. She bought medical books about diabetes and began studying. Every book said there is no cure for juvenile diabetes. She read in the *American Diabetes Association Complete Guide to Diabetes* that pancreas transplants were showing some promise, but for now, the only viable treatment for the type of diabetes Sergei had was insulin. Another book said that the blindness and kidney failure often associated with diabetes could result *from* taking insulin.

"That was contradictory, and it strengthened my decision to not put him on insulin," Victoria recalls.

The doctor said he would report Victoria to Child Protective Services if she didn't put Sergei on insulin. The threat of having her child taken away made her frantic to find a solution. With no help from the medical profession or medical books, she decided to do her own research, not in

219

a medical lab, but on the streets. If she could not find a scientific solution, she would find an anecdotal one.

Victoria noticed that some people look run-down and sluggish, while others look vibrant and healthy. She overcame her shyness and began walking up to healthy-looking strangers, asking whether they knew of a cure for diabetes. Standing in line at a bank one day, she noticed the woman in front of her seemed radiant.

"Do you know of a cure for diabetes?" Victoria asked.

"Of course," the woman responded. "The body can heal everything."

The two stood outside the bank and talked for an hour. The woman, Elisabeth, explained that she had cured her colon cancer more than a decade earlier by switching to a diet in which no foods are cooked, all are raw.

Raw food advocates say that cooking destroys the nutritive elements of food—the vitamins, minerals and enzymes—and that cooked and processed foods clog the digestive system, resulting in a wide variety of illnesses.

"I was shocked. It was radical, but I felt it made sense," Victoria recalls. And just as her intuition had told here there was a cure for diabetes, her intuition also told her this cure would work. "I trusted my intuition, because I didn't have anything else to trust," she said.

Victoria immediately went to the bookstore to learn more. But she couldn't find any books about raw food diets. It was the first roadblock, but she didn't give up. She began writing to health institutes asking for information. Finally, she found a few books on the subject. But then she hit roadblock number two: her husband, Igor.

"He didn't want to go on raw foods. He said he'd divorce me. He couldn't imagine his life without Russian food," Victoria recalls. "He said, 'If it's so simple, all the doctors would recommend it.'"

Victoria didn't know what to do. Her intuition told her that for Sergei to successfully stick to a raw food diet, the whole family would have to eat that way.

"Then we got lucky; my husband got very sick," Victoria says. Illness, she says, can be a stroke of luck when it leads us to actions that will improve our health. Igor was diagnosed with a thyroid problem. The doctor said he would have to remove Igor's thyroid gland and put him on hormones. Wanting to avoid the operation, Igor agreed to try a raw food diet—but only for two weeks.

"It was January 21, 1994. That day I threw out all the pots and pans, the toaster, the microwave. I cleaned out the refrigerator," Victoria recalls. "I sliced pears and apples and oranges, because I didn't know what else to do."

And for the next two weeks, the family felt like they were starving.

"At first, everyone really suffered from being hungry. But within two days, everyone started feeling better. And within two weeks, the major symptoms went away." Victoria says.

Sergei's blood sugar level dropped and stabilized.[1] His sister, Valya, had suffered from asthma her entire life, and she suddenly stopped wheezing and choking at night. Igor's hands stopped shaking, and his pulse dropped from one hundred and seventy to one hundred and ten beats per minute. And Victoria's heart stopped its sporadic pattern of beats and pauses.

Victoria had found her cure, not only for diabetes, but also for arrhythmia and thyroid dysfunction and asthma. She found it neither in medical books nor in a doctor's office, but from another human being. Anecdotal evidence—so disparaged by the medical community as unscientific—had put Victoria's entire family on the path back to health. It's a path that leads away from a lifetime of illness and reliance on the medical establishment. It's a path the leads toward self-empowerment and a path that leads to life.

Are You Addicted to Cooked Food?

After beginning to teach others the health benefits of eating raw foods, Victoria noticed that most people were very excited by the information and committed to changing to a raw-food lifestyle. But almost no one stuck with it permanently.

Victoria spent more than a year trying to figure out why. Then one day, attending an Alcoholics Anonymous meeting with a friend, it struck her: People are addicted to cooked food.

Victoria has now developed a twelve-step program that enables people who want to be raw fooders to live free of cooked foods.

The program is outlined in her book, *12 Steps to Raw Foods: How to End Your Addiction to Cooked Food*. It also is taught at two-day workshops and three-day retreats around the country. For a schedule of retreats, go to www.rawfamily.com.

Chapter 48

Kim Dunn Becomes
Her Own Guinea Pig

Doing your own research is not enough. You're going to have to put what you learn into action. No doctor will provide you with the tools. This isn't what he was taught to do in medical school. He could lose his license. So you're going to have to get everything yourself.

Kim Dunn's personality and profession prepared her well to take action, relying on her own judgment. She was, after all, an attorney and later a judge. She was used to a systematic and logical thought process. She was confident in her ability to quickly absorb the information needed to make a good decision.

So when a blood test showed she had the Epstein-Barr virus, and when the doctors offered no cure, Kim immediately began gathering information. She turned first to the Internet. She learned that almost everyone has the Epstein-Barr virus in their bloodstreams, but it's latent. She reasoned that the virus would have remained latent in her if her immune system had been strong.

"The immune system can conquer almost anything if it's healthy. If you bombard it in a variety of ways with repeated challenges, it will diminish and become too weak to fight anything, then you'll get ill. So I asked, 'What's out there that can be harming my immune system?'"

She went back to the Internet for answers. She organized the information she gleaned into categories and put together what she calls the "portfolio approach." An investor will combine several stocks in a portfolio, knowing that some will lose and some will gain, but overall, the portfolio should improve. In the same way, a good health-recovery program can contain many treatments, at least some of which are likely to work.

But there's one big difference between stocks and health treatments. When a stock goes up, everyone who owns it earns the same amount per share, whereas a health treatment will affect each person in a different way. "What people need to understand is that everyone's different. What works for one person may not work for another," Kim says. That's one reason to try a variety of things that have worked for other people—to act as your own guinea pig. You must be your own test subject, because you are the only one who will react your specific way to a specific remedy.

Just to cover all her bases, Kim tried six treatments and lifestyle changes.

First, she changed her diet. She bought *Prescription for Nutritional Healing* and other nutritional health books. "I had no idea just how adulterated and toxic the foods are that we eat today," Kim said. "They are genetically mutated and contain hormones, antibiotics, pesticides, gluten, sugar, etcetera." So she eliminated canned foods and began eating mostly green and fresh organic vegetables.

Second, she used the Beck zapper to kill the Epstein-Barr virus. She had heard about zappers from her mother's friend. She researched the specifications and had one built. During the first four weeks of use, her fatigue increased instead of getting better. "But after a month, I couldn't believe the change in my energy level. I could go from six a.m. to eleven p.m. every day without a nap. It blew me away. I never felt that way in my whole life." If she stopped using the zapper, her symptoms returned.

Third, she drank colloidal silver, also to kill the virus. Instead of paying thirty dollars per four-ounce bottle from the health-food store, she built a colloidal silver maker for fifteen dollars and could then make silver water herself for pennies a glass. The very first day she drank the silver water, she noticed an improvement in her health. She has since developed her own theory about why colloidal silver works to kill microorganisms.

Fourth, she borrowed a magnetic mattress and slept on it. The first night, she slept deeply. And the next day, she didn't have to take her customary nap. Instead of buying such a mattress for four hundred dollars, she made her own, calibrating and gluing thirty bar magnets onto a mattress-size piece of egg-crate foam.

Fifth, she reduced her exposure to harmful electromagnetic fields. Her research into zappers and magnets had taught her that some types of electrical fields are beneficial to the human body and others are harmful. She learned that alternating-current fields at more than two milligauss are harmful to living organisms. "This isn't the standard outlined by the government, but it is generally accepted by people who have written books about these health hazards," Kim says. She had the local power company come to her house to measure the fields. Many power companies provide this service for free, sending someone out to run a meter over appliances, vehicles and outside wires. In Kim's house, the meter showed her treadmill putting out eight milligauss at chest level and her microwave putting out five hundred milligauss. Kim replaced the electric treadmill with a manual one and began unplugging the microwave when not in use.

Sixth, she eliminated chemicals from her water and air. Instead of drinking city water, which contains "acceptable levels" of deadly chemicals used to kill organisms in the water, Kim started buying reverse-osmosis water. She made her cleaning lady stop using chemical cleaners, and she stopped using fertilizers and pesticides in her yard.

Accomplishing everything in her portfolio—and doing it long enough to have an impact on her health—took more than a year. But by the end of 1999, Kim felt as if the virus was beginning to leave her body. Little by little, she slowly regained her health.

Like so many people who are recovering from chronic ailments, she suffered a setback. During the time that she was recovering from her illness, she had two surgeries—a hysterectomy and an operation on her shoulder.

"They were insistent about loading me up with drugs, mixing several at a time—drugs I didn't want or need. That was huge, trying to explain to the doctors and nurses not to give me drugs without my knowledge," Kim says. "Ironically, when I needed my pain medications, they were nowhere to be found." Kim found it so difficult to remain in charge of decisions impacting her body that she determined to not fall into the medical system again. "I now live a healthy lifestyle so I can avoid hospitals and the medical system in general. I no longer have to argue with them about what's best for me."

After the operations, in the spring of 2001, her old symptoms started coming back. She was discouraged, but at least she didn't have to start from square one.

"I thought, I got better once before, let's revisit all the things I did before."

She went back to eating organic green vegetables. She also suspected electromagnetic fields as a culprit, and this time she bought her own meter so she could eliminate or avoid harmful fields.

"Avoidance doesn't cost a whole lot, so why not?" Kim says. "A lot of people thought I was a weirdo, but I got rid of cell phones and touch lamps and speaker phones and cleaned all the potentially dangerous devices out of my house."

She felt somewhat better but knew she hadn't yet finished the job.

"Really focusing on how you're feeling allows you to begin figuring out what's impacting your health negatively," she says.

She researched her symptoms and noticed many were listed as symptoms of diabetes. Finally, she decided to bring a couple of health-care practitioners in to help. She covered all her bases, making appointments with both a medical doctor and a naturopathic physician.

"The MD made me feel like she was in a big hurry. I'd made a list of my symptoms. She said, 'You've listed three of the five symptoms of depression.' She said I might need an anti-depressant. I said, 'I'll keep that in mind, but please just run the blood test for diabetes.' MDs are very myopic. You have to be insistent and tell them what you want."

"The naturopath listened to my symptoms and asked questions and wrote down the answers and conducted tests right then and there in her office. In one such test, she had me lie down and then quickly stand up. When I stood up, my blood pressure dropped thirty points; it's supposed to rise about ten points. The naturopath found that my adrenals were exhausted and said, 'Let's look at your food intolerances.' She gave me adrenal supplements and found intolerances to dairy, fruit and sugar."

Kim's blood test showed she was glucose intolerant. The MD and ND came to the same conclusion: Kim had an abnormally low level of blood sugar. She was hypoglycemic.

So she changed her diet again, eliminating all but organic meats and vegetables. And she decided to get the amalgam fillings removed from her teeth.

"Mercury is more toxic than lead, so what the hell are they doing putting it in our mouths?" Kim asks.

"When I get the fillings taken out of my teeth, I'll be optimistic that I've done everything possible to build back my immune system," she said a month before the first dentist appointment. "I've always been an intense person doing three things at once. I'll know I'm back to full health when I can do three things at once all day from seven a.m. to ten p.m." She says that on a scale of zero to ten, her health had been at zero and is now at eight.

Kim attributes her recovery to all the treatments and protocols in her portfolio, particularly diet. She's considered writing a book to share what she's learned in the process of being her own guinea pig.

"Most people don't have the time to get educated or the money to try all these things. I've considered writing a book to help others. You can't say, 'This is a cure.' You have to disclaim it. But it could say, 'Here are the things you have to look at: diet, electromagnetic fields, mercury fillings, etcetera.'"

"The most important thing is to be open minded about what all types of alternative medicine have to offer," Kim says, "because you have nothing to lose and everything to gain."

The Bioelectric Body

Just as polluted water can harm us and pure water can help heal us, electromagnetic pollution can harm us while electrical currents can help heal us.

The best source of information about both is the book *Cross Currents: The Promise of Electromedicine, the Perils of Electropollution*, by Robert O. Becker, an orthopedic surgeon nominated twice for the Nobel Prize.

Three of the methods Kim used to cure herself—the Beck zapper, magnet therapy and elimination of harmful electrical waves—are related to electromagnetic fields.

- **The Beck Zapper:** In the early 1990s, scientists at the Albert Einstein College of Medicine noticed that electricity deactivated HIV in a petri dish. They came up with the idea of a machine that would be similar to a kidney dialysis machine. It would take the blood out of the body, run an electric current through it, then put it back in. Physicist Robert Beck invented a less invasive alternative—a small battery-operated device that electrifies the blood while it's in the body. It does this using electrodes placed over artery pulse points. For information, type the words "Beck zapper" into any Internet search engine.

- **Magnet therapy:** Magnets are thought to improve health by attracting and repelling charged particles in the blood, which increases circulation for quicker healing. The electrical current created by magnets stimulates the nervous system in a way that reduces pain, perhaps by stimulating the release of endorphins, the body's natural painkiller. Magnets may also improve health by organizing the body's subtle energy fields.

228

• **Electromagnetic pollution:** The random electrical fields bombarding us from power lines, transformers, kitchen appliances, overhead lighting, cell phones and a myriad of other electrical devices may contribute to diseases ranging from cancer to chronic fatigue. The Environmental Protection Agency began reviewing studies of electromagnetic fields (EMFs) in the late 1980s. In 1990, it issued a draft report recommending EMFs be classified a carcinogen. After release of the report, pressure from special interests caused the EPA to add a caveat saying, "The basic nature of the interaction between EMFs and biological processes leading to cancer is not understood."

Chapter 49

Jeff Houck Takes the Guesswork Out of Self-Treatment

Jeff Houck is living proof that you can take charge of your own health and be your own healer; that you can experiment on yourself with various treatments and cure your own illness.

But Jeff has an advantage that most people don't have. He knows how to take the guesswork out of self-diagnosis and treatment. He learned a way to ask the body questions and get answers from it. This method is called applied kinesiology—more informally called muscle testing. Without it, Jeff may have never gotten a correct diagnosis. With it, he not only solved the puzzle of what was wrong, he knew exactly what to prescribe for himself.

Before learning kinesiology, Jeff had to rely solely on research and experimentation. The trial-and-error method worked, but it was time consuming. For his allergies, he had to read all about vitamins and minerals. Then he had to experiment with various combinations. Over a six-year period, he learned, for example, that vitamin B will not control his allergies unless he adds vitamin C and bioflavonoids. He no longer had to take antihistamines for his runny nose and scratchy eyes, but it took more than half a decade of experimentation to get there.

Then he learned kinesiology. His ability to treat himself increased exponentially. As a biologist and former nursing school student, he was well acquainted with the scientific method. So after he learned about kinesiology, he set up several experiments to determine whether it really worked.

"The scientific method is simply a five-step problem-solving process," he says. "My wife and I tested the accuracy of muscle testing by doing as close to double-blind studies as we could."

They put various substances in look-alike brown papers bags. Some substances were toxic to the body, some beneficial. Then they set up a series of experiments to find out whether their muscles would always be weakened when holding a bag with a toxic substance and always be strengthened when holding a bag with a healthy substance. In this way, they discovered the body's wisdom—that the body knows what will hurt or heal it better than the mind does.

Jeff has used kinesiology to help cure various ailments over the years, including shingles and congested kidneys. He also went to chiropractors and a naturopath for assistance in his healing journey. The things that worked for him include:

- Quitting a high-stress job. This cut Jeff's need for vitamins.
- Drinking fresh lemon juice to break up kidney stones.
- Taking yellow dock, parsley and corn silk to clear his kidneys.
- Using raw maple syrup as a substitute for sugar.
- Taking cayenne pepper to improve his metabolism.
- Taking B-complex vitamins and vitamin C with bioflavonoids.
- Taking lecithin to support the myelin sheath surrounding the nerves.
- Using the system developed by naturopath Hulda Clark to rid his body of parasites. After using this parasite cleanse, Jeff discovered through kinesiology that his body's need for vitamins had plummeted.
- Drinking a product called Willard Water™ that helps the body assimilate nutrients. Jeff explains Willard Water's molecular makeup in scientific terms, but for the purpose of explaining it to the layman, he describes it simply as "wetter water."
- Taking melatonin and niacin for better sleep at night and as an antioxidant. Melatonin is a hormone produced by the pineal gland as a response to darkness. It creates sleepiness and improves the quality of sleep.
- Taking MSM to maintain the joints. Methylsulfonylmethane works by supplying the mineral sulfer, which is used by virtually all protein

molecules in the body. MSM supplements are most often used as an anti-inflammatory to help reduce arthritis, muscle and joint pain.

- Using cold-pressed coconut oil as an anti-microbial. Jeff explains that it breaks down into monolaurin, which will kill any virus encapsulated in lipids. "It's used for shingles and is very promising for AIDS," he says.

- Using a Rife machine to treat shingles. Shingles is caused by the herpes zoster virus—the same virus that causes chicken pox, Jeff explains. All people have the virus, but it usually remains latent, only causing symptoms when something activates it. Then, it infects the nerve sheath, inflaming it and causing severe pain. "Being viral, allopathic medicine says there's nothing we can do to kill the virus. That's an overstatement. There's no antibiotic, but there are herbs that can kill a virus, including cats claw and elderberry as well as coconut oil. And Rife frequencies kill viruses as well," Jeff says. A Rife machine is a frequency generation device. Various frequencies kill various pathogens, so the machine is set to the frequency range of whatever virus, parasite or bacterium is causing the problem.

- Drinking ionized water. A naturopath had suggested Jeff's tissues might be too acidic. So Jeff bought a water filter with an ionizer, which makes the water alkaline. After a month of drinking a gallon a day of the ionized water, his pain began going away. "All the pain was in the muscle, and I think it was essentially uric acid build-up," Jeff says. "The body will sequester acids in the soft tissues; they're acidic body wastes that would usually be processed off by the kidneys. This causes muscles to go spastic and cramp."

When people ask him what they can do to improve their health, Jeff suggests they drink a gallon of water a day, use coconut oil, sleep longer hours, use MSM for joint problems, and take a vitamin B complex and vitamin C with bioflavinoids. "For severely ill people, they need liver and colon and gall bladder cleanses. Detoxify the filtering system of the body, and then it will start working again," he says.

Jeff's combination of herbs, natural substances, bioelectric medicine and stress reduction was customized specifically for his body type, blood type, past medical history and current medical condition—not by some sophisticated computer program, but by his body itself, via kinesiology.

"The thing I can't stress enough is to learn how to muscle test so you can customize your treatment protocol. The body is dynamic, always changing, so muscle test often," Jeff says. "When I first started treating my illnesses, it was hit and miss, a very slow process. With muscle testing, you're right on target, and your overall health improves."

Today, Jeff is nearly pain-free. "I brought myself up from woefully bad to a manageable state," he says. "A year ago, I didn't think I'd ever be able to work again. I returned to the fish hatchery three months ago. We move two-hundred-pound screens, and I have no fear of my back going out."

Jeff's Recommended Reading List

Jeff recommends the following books for people who want to learn more about the methods he used to heal. He learned of these books on an Internet bulletin board about alternative medicine. Go to http://groups.yahoo.com and search for Mr Tracys Corner—with that exact punctuation.

- *Your Body's Many Cries for Water*, by Fereydoon Batmanghelidj.
- *What's Really Wrong With You: A Revolutionary Look at How Muscles Affect Your Health*, by Thomas Griner with Maxine Nunes.
- *The Cure for All Diseases*, by Hulda Clark, ND.
- *The Healing Miracles of Coconut Oil*, by Bruce Fife, ND.
- *Know Your Fats: The Complete Primer for Understanding the Nutrition of Fats, Oils and Cholesterol*, by Mary G. Enig.
- *The Carbohydrate Addict's Lifespan Program: A Personalized Plan for Becoming Slim, Fit and Healthy in Your 40s, 50s, 60s and Beyond*, by Dr. Rachael F. Heller, et al.
- *Lights Out: Sleep, Sugar and Survival*, by T.S. Wiley.
- *Melatonin: Your Body's Natural Wonder Drug*, by Russel J. Reiter and Jo Robinson.
- *Touch for Health*, by John F. Thie, DC.

Applied Kinesiology

In 1964, Dr. George Goodheart, a Detroit chiropractor, developed applied kinesiology—a method of testing the strength of muscles to evaluate neurological functions. Today, it is used by numerous chiropractors, doctors and dentists to diagnose structural and organic problems.

Muscle testing does not measure the amount of strength a muscle has, but rather how the nervous system is controlling muscle function. The indicator muscle supplies information via nerve pathways, providing a way to access the mind-body connection.

Adept practitioners can ask the body questions to get an accurate diagnosis. For example, if you knew kinesiology and were experiencing pain in the lower abdomen, you could muscle test yourself while asking, "Is this pain caused by a bladder infection?" With practice, you can learn to feel when the body says "yes."

A good starting place to learn about kinesiology or to find out where you can receive training is the Web site www.kinesiology.net.

Here's a simple experiment you can do to see how it works: Hold something that is good for your health, such as an organic vegetable, in your right hand. Hold your left arm out straight to the side. Have your partner push down at your wrist. Notice whether it is easy to resist the pressure. How strong does your arm and shoulder feel? Now, hold something that is bad for your health, such as cigarettes or sugar, and have your partner push down on your outstretched arm. Do you seem to have the same strength to resist? Have fun with it. Test everything in your kitchen. Soon, you'll know exactly what your body does or does not want.

Chapter 50

Darla Greenig and the Try-Everything Approach

Darla Greenig is living proof that alternative medicines and treatments are usually safe. She's tried so many, she can't even remember them all. But she does remember slowly healing to wellness.

After more than a decade of pain, fatigue and insomnia, a rheumatologist diagnosed fibromyalgia. He said he could do no more than offer her pain pills. But Darla had a daughter-in-law with fibromyalgia who had been helped by a clinic in Fort Collins, Colorado, so Darla decided to go.

The clinic began by prescribing homeopathic remedies. They didn't help. So she went to another alternative clinic—this one in Billings, Montana. It screened for all pathogens, and found that Darla had several, including candida, grain mold and intestinal flukes. She also had numerous toxins stored in her tissues, ranging from solvents to heavy metals.

"They gave me hope, but I was so tired of being tired," Darla recalls. There was much she would have to do to get well, and the thought of all that effort nearly defeated her.

"I said to my husband, 'I feel like I'm sinking. I'm going down for the third time, and I'm too tired to do the things they want me to.' With fibromyalgia, you don't think clearly. I have an active mind and can organize things well, yet I couldn't even come up with the words I wanted to use."

Still, she had to continue searching for a cure. Her sister and brother-in-law, Cheryl and Ken, invited her to stay with them in Salt Lake City for

237

the start of her healing journey. "Ken said, 'Darla, we can beat this.' That's what I needed. I started feeling better just because I had hope."

She also began researching autoimmune diseases and health. "I read and read and read while I was able. I didn't have the Internet, so I went to the library." She took a class in medicinal herbs and talked to a few natural health practitioners. Then she began experimenting.

"We have a God-given mind and body, and there were things that I knew intuitively through my spirit were good for me to take for healing."

She listened to her body, noticing how it felt after she ate certain foods. Then she began eating only those foods that seemed to support her body and increase her energy. She made tinctures from herbs that clean the kidneys, liver and blood. She took herbs that clean the colon, and she enhanced its functioning with acidophilus supplements. She stopped drinking unfiltered tap water and started taking vitamins and minerals. She used cayenne pepper to reduce her blood pressure and took an herb from Africa that increases serotonin in the brain to improve her sleep. She tried magnets as well as two kinds of bioelectric zappers. She ingested a type of hydrogen as an anti-oxidant and drank Essiac tea.

"I did the shotgun approach," Darla says. "I would not necessarily advise it, but I was so desirous of becoming well that I tried a lot of things at once."

And she noticed that gradually, she was feeling better and better. Today, although she's not pain-free, she feels eighty percent better.

She now believes that numerous root canals—which may trap bacteria and release toxins—led to her illness. Because she has eight or nine, she assumes she'll have to have her teeth removed in order to completely heal, but she can't yet afford the eight thousand to ten thousand dollars it would cost. "My insurance won't touch this," she said. She believes she will one day have the money to fix the dental culprit. Meanwhile, she continues to try new therapies that she hears about.

"I was told I should never dismiss any therapy, and I've lived by that," Darla says. But she's dismayed that she's one of the few who does.

"I don't even tell people anymore about alternative remedies, because I get these blank stares. I honestly had a friend turn away when I told her, 'You don't have to have that gall bladder operation.' She looked away from me and at a friend, and I know that they were thinking, 'Darla's gone over the edge.'"

People who have healed themselves from chronic illness through years of study and experimentation soon learn that the knowledge they have gained is valued only by people who are willing to take responsibility for their health.

It's a small group, indeed, and Darla feels fortunate to be one of its members.

Is it Fibromyalgia?

Fibromyalgia is characterized by fatigue and widespread pain or stiffness in several areas of the body. It may be accompanied by difficulty sleeping, chronic headaches, swollen joints, irritable bowel syndrome and numbness or tingling sensations. Possible causes are toxins accumulating in the muscles, low levels of serotonin, candida overgrowth, nutritional deficiencies, a malfunctioning thyroid or adrenal gland, mercury poisoning from amalgam fillings and the Epstein-Barr virus.

An excellent source for detailed information on fibromyalgia—its symptoms, causes and cures—is www.holistic-online.com. Click on "fibromyalgia" under the "Diseases and Remedies" section.

Chapter 51

Linda Pranzitelli Finds Meaning in Illness

There are many worse things than dying. Dying is easy. It's facing illness—doing what you have to do with dignity and character—that requires far more of you. Just to survive, period, is much harder than dying."

That's what Linda Pranzitelli concluded after struggling to heal from a stroke in 1995 and later getting Crohn's disease. And yet she also believes that illness can be a blessing in disguise.

When the doctor said he could do nothing for Linda's Crohn's disease, Linda decided to get a second opinion—this one from a naturopath who told Linda she had the classic symptoms of candida overgrowth.

"She said, 'You've had it a long time and it will take a long time to get over it, but I promise you if you work with this, over a year or a year and a half, we can have you well."

The naturopath prescribed acidophilus, vitamin C, berberine sulfate, gentian, garlic, ginger root, quassia root and nystatin. To reduce the pains in her joints, Linda drank apple cider vinegar mixed with honey.

And she didn't tell her allopathic doctor about it. "I don't want to hear what he has to say," she explained. "When I was young, I overheard my obstetrician in a room with a woman. He said, 'When you're prescribed a medicine, don't stop taking it. Either you do what I say, or you don't come in. You're wasting my time and your money.' I agree with him. If I trust you enough with my health to come to you, I have to do what you say. Why go if you're not going to do what he says? Try the MD, do what he says; if it doesn't work, then move on."

That's what Linda did, and her symptoms began improving. She combines natural and allopathic treatments based on which work best for her.

Because of her religious ilk, she sees meaning in her illness, finding a positive side to the suffering. "Afflictions keep you close to the Lord," she says.

She has also used her disease to improve herself.

"Being ill has changed me. I've learned to let go. I've stopped trying to control things and other people. I've learned to depend on God," Linda says. "Illness is the proverbial blessing in disguise."

242

Healed and Transformed

Few books are available about the transformative aspect of illness in general. Many books, such as *Heartsearch: Toward Healing Lupus*, tell the story of one person's fight with a particular disease, and how that person was transformed, whether cured or still ill. Many others discuss how life's ordeals—physical or emotional—can lead to spiritual growth and a stronger sense of meaning. But few talk about how healing transforms people healed from chronic or deadly illness.

One that comes close is *The Wounded Storyteller: Body, Illness, and Ethics*. Author Arthur Frank outlines three types of illness narratives, including "quest" narratives. People with quest stories, he explains, used their illness to become someone new.

Chapter 52

Thomas Deer and the Three Healers

Various healing substances and therapeutic devices are credited with curing a wide range of diseases. They treat the physical body, supporting and balancing its natural healing systems and deactivating or devitalizing pathogens that interfere with healing. But treating the physical body is only part of the healing game. And when you're fighting for your life, you want to cover all the bases.

That's why Thomas Deer wasn't satisfied simply with taking herbs for his cancer. You'll recall that his cancer had moved from his kidneys to his lungs, and with a ten-month life sentence from the doctor, he had been preparing to die. But then a friend from his Trout Unlimited group suggested he drink Essiac tea.

So Thomas went to the Internet, researched Essiac and decided to give it a try. He also decided to take shark cartilage supplements after hearing about how a colleague's father had eliminated his lung cancer with shark cartilage. Since then, Thomas' tumors have been shrinking. The ten months has long passed, and he's still alive.

"I think if you can cure things with nature, you're better off," Thomas says.

But he went beyond researching natural healing substances. He also went to the library and checked out audiotapes such as *Success Through Relaxation* and *Strengthen Your Immune System*. As a supervisor at Kimberly-Clarke, he had attended motivational classes, which taught him that you usually achieve what you believe you can.

"I believe your mind can do an awful lot," Thomas says. "I'm a firm believer that my immune system can kill this."

To help maintain that positive attitude, he retired from his job to avoid stress. "If you don't give your body anything else to fight, then it can fight the cancer," he explains.

The third part of his healing equation was prayer. He asked all his friends and family to pray for his healing. "I bet the Lord is tired of hearing my name," he says, adding that he believes his faith is doing more to cure him than anything else.

Thomas doesn't care whether it's herbs, attitude, divine intervention or a combination of all three curing his cancer. His doctor said, "I don't know what you're doing, but keep doing it." And he is.

He suffered a setback in January 2002 when he learned he also had tumors in his bladder. But the news did not set him back emotionally.

"I really feel like the bladder cancer is going to be easy to control. I feel like I'm winning," he said. "I feel positive enough that we just bought a couple of acres."

In his early retirement, he's enjoyed life immensely, spending time traveling, fishing and teaching kids to tie flies. "I told my wife, 'The day I decide to die, you'll see me walk in the house with a big old cigar, because that's the thing I miss the most.'"

Tom doesn't expect to ever smoke a cigar again.

More About Positive Attitude and Prayer

The following is a sampling of the many good books available about prayer as it relates to healing and about positive thinking.
- *The Isaiah Effect: Decoding the Lost Science of Prayer and Prophecy*, by Gregg Braden.
- *Healing Words: The Power of Prayer and the Practice of Medicine*, and *Prayer Is Good Medicine: How to Reap the Healing Benefits of Prayer*, both by Larry Dossey, MD.
- *Love, Medicine and Miracles: Lessons Learned About Self-Healing from a Surgeon's Experience With Exceptional Patients*, by Bernie S. Siegel, MD.
- *The Power of Positive Thinking*, by Norman Vincent Peale.

How to Buy or Make Essiac Tea

Essiac tea can be purchased at most health food stores already brewed and bottled. A money-saving option is to buy the dry herbs pre-mixed from Tehachapi Tea Company, then brew them yourself. Tehachapi Tea Company can be reached at www.anursesherbaltea.com or 1-800-843-2181. If you'd like to buy the dried herbs separately and mix them yourself, here's the recipe:

Mix together:
    4.25 oz. Burdock root
    2.8 oz. Sheep sorrel
    0.7 oz. Slippery elm bark
    0.18 oz. Turkey rhubarb root

Bring two gallons of water to a boil. Stir in the herbs. Continue to boil at reduced heat for 10 minutes with lid on. Turn stove off. Let sit for 12 hours. Reheat, but do not bring to a boil. Strain out the herbs and store the remaining liquid in bottles in the refrigerator.

Drink at least two ounces three times daily on an empty stomach, cold or heated. Do not heat in a microwave oven.

(If you search the Internet for more information about Essiac, you will find a raging debate over who has the real recipe used by Renee Caisse, after whom Essiac was named. Caisse learned the formula from the Ojibwa Indians. A naturopath of Ojibwa descent told Cynthia Olsen, author of *Essiac: A Native Herbal Cancer Remedy*, that the argument over the exact recipe is silly. He said he makes the tea using "a big handful" of one ingredient and a "wad" of another. He suggests drinking eight ounces or more a day. For stubborn tumors, he suggests adding bloodroot tincture.)

Where to Start

When you're ready to do your own research, a good starting place is the World Research Foundation. For about seventy dollars, it will send you hundreds of pages of information about your specific medical problem culled from its twenty-five-thousand-book library. Visit the foundation at www.wrf.org, or call 928-284-3300.

Chapter 53

Trail Guides

The self-healers you've just read about decided to share the stories of their journeys back to health. In doing so, they have agreed to be your trail guides.

But the path back to health has a thousand branch-off trails, and each self-healer in this book has taken only one—a trail that led to the desired destination, but still, only one trail branching off of the path.

The wisdom they have gained on the journey tells them that their particular paths—the particular substances or spiritual practices or health-care systems that worked for them—may not be the right ones for you. Their examples are meant only to inspire; they're not meant to outline the perfect healing protocol for everyone.

Still, there are things that most of their healing journeys had in common. And so the stories you have just read can let you know what you're likely to encounter no matter which branch of the path you take. The self-healers' stories can point to the common stumbling blocks on the healing path. And the stories can let you know what tools you can use to turn those stumbling blocks into stepping stones.

Let's review both the stumbling blocks and the useful tools.

Stumbling Block 1: The Length of the Trail

Dr. Bernie Siegel always asked his patients why they thought they healed. He discovered they did not experience spontaneous remissions, but that they worked hard to overcome illness.

Some of the self-healers in this book started their healing journeys five or more years ago, and they're still not at the end of the trail. They've worked hard, researching, experimenting, changing habits of thought and action. They're making progress, they feel much better, they have energy again and can live normal or nearly normal lives. But they're not done.

Toughing it out over the long haul is tough. When you feel yourself making progress, that makes it easier. You get the sense you're doing the right thing, and that motivates you to keep on keeping on. But don't fool yourself that a few herbs and organic foods and positive-thought tapes are going to cure you quickly. It took many years or even decades to get this sick, and it may take years to return to full health.

What makes the trail longer is the fact that you may have to heal not one, but several, problems. The self-healers often refer to this as "peeling the onion."

For example, using grapefruit seed extract to rid the body of excess candida may eliminate the overgrowth. But that's only the first step. Next, you'll have to find a way to get rid of the build-up of encrusted mucous lining the walls of your colon. Once this is accomplished, you'll be absorbing nutrients again and your energy will return. But now you may find that you still have to deal with the toxins you've breathed, eaten and absorbed through your skin over the years—toxins that the body has been unable to eliminate. Perhaps you'll choose juice fasts to take care of this. Now that the candida is back in balance, the bowel is functioning and old toxins are cleaned out, you may find that you still fall back into periods of fatigue and difficulty concentrating. So what now?

You've already had to do a lot to get this far. And you've had to give up a lot, too. You had to stop eating sugar and wheat. You gave up coffee and alcohol. You quit your high-paying job for one with less stress. Just when you thought you were done with all the work it takes to heal, you find you're still not at the end of the journey. You wish you were the Energizer™ bunny with batteries that keep going and going and going.

You have to keep going, because you've come this far, and you can't turn back now. What's the alternative? A lifetime of chronic fatigue? Or perhaps the end of a lifetime?

So you go back to the drawing board. You do more research. You learn it may help to have an old root canal removed. And then you find your liver is weak from the heavy load of toxins it's had to clean out over the years, so you need to take milk-thistle-seed extract to rebuild it. After three years of healing work, you're still not done.

Many naturopaths will tell you it takes about a month to heal for every year you've been sick. The problem is, many of us have been sick for decades and just don't know it until it progresses to chronic fatigue or cancer or heart disease.

The penicillin you took at age three for an ear infection initially threw your bowel flora out of balance, allowing the candida to thrive. The antibiotic-treated meat you've been eating ever since has maintained the imbalance. Now you're forty, and a stressful home life has increased the imbalance, leading to systemic candida and chronic fatigue. You've been getting sick for four decades, and it may take four years to reverse the damage and heal.

Holistic healers also will tell you about healing crises. After you've taken ten steps forward on your healing path, suddenly, you'll seem to take five back. Your ever-increasing energy level will plummet. Or you'll get severe diarrhea for a week. These healing crises are particularly heart wrenching when the path seems so long. This is the time when it helps to be working with a holistic health-care practitioner who knows all about healing crises and can reassure you they're a natural and necessary part of the journey back to wellness.

Without that kind of support, you might trip over...

Stumbling Block 2: It's Lonely at the Fringe

If you're living in Europe or one of the many countries that allow all medical modalities to compete openly in the marketplace, you won't be on the fringe. But here in the United States, what you're doing is called everything from "alternative" to "crazy."

The FDA is out to stop it. No one you know has any experience with it. Your friends look at you a little funny when you tell them what you're doing. Your family encourages you to "just do what the doctor says."

And your doctor says your alternative cure won't work. In fact, he may even tell you he can no longer be your doctor, because he fears your actions will jeopardize his malpractice insurance coverage. He certainly won't cooperate or offer advice related to your self-treatment. He could lose his license to practice medicine if he did.

Remember Tricia Bies? Remember how she was afraid to go to the doctor after her self-treatment caused her tumor to fall out, so she put a colander over the deep wound, not knowing what else to do? The doctor hinted she had made the situation worse, saying, "Because you've done this thing, there's nothing I can sew to that." He refused her offer to bring in the tumor for him to examine, completely uninterested in this near-miracle of a person removing her own tumor. The oncologist used guilt to try to convince her to take chemotherapy, saying, "If you don't do it for yourself, do it for your children." The surgeon who replaced her laetrie catheter wouldn't advise her on what kind of bandage to use, saying, "I don't really care how you dress it."

It's difficult to both go to a medical doctor and continue with a healing regimen that the doctor did not recommend. It's truly lonely at the fringe.

And because here in the United States, natural medicine is pushed to the fringe, you'll also run into...

Stumbling Block 3: The High Cost of Healing

Actually, natural medicine is much less expensive than the invasive, high-tech methods and chemicals used by allopathic medicine. But most insurance companies won't cover it, so the expense comes out of your pocket.

Studies show that between sixty and seventy-five percent of the cost for unconventional care is paid by the patient.

This has begun to change. Many insurance companies now cover treatment provided by two types of alternative practitioners: naturopathic doctors and chiropractors. But there are dozens of other healing practices —herbology, Reiki, iridology, reflexology and polarity therapy, to name a few. Unless you use one of the most progressive insurance carriers, you'll have to pay for treatment from these professionals yourself.

If you do your own research and treat yourself, no insurance company will pay for that. So if you're convinced that a Rife machine will cure your prostate cancer, be ready to fork out a thousand dollars to buy it yourself. Buying acidophilus to restore a balance of good bacteria in your colon may cost twenty dollars a bottle, but it's not a prescription, so it comes out of your own wallet. Getting amalgam fillings removed from your teeth is not recognized by the medical monopoly as necessary for good health, so you'll have to pay for that yourself.

With so many reasons not to embark on a healing journey, with so many stumbling blocks on the path, it helps to have...

Useful Tool 1: A Health-Care Practitioner Parter

It doesn't matter whether he is a nutritional counselor, a holistic MD (their numbers are growing), an energy healer, a homeopathist or a naturopath—just someone who spends his time helping others heal.

How do you find this someone? You can look in the phone book. You can get a referral from friends. You can ask at the health food store. You can read the ads in the alternative press. But start somewhere. Go to someone.

Better yet, go to several. Remember how Linda Koep's chiropractor put together a team of health-care practitioners to help her? Remember how Annie Wilkin went to nearly a dozen different healing professionals before she found one who did more than make mild improvements in her condition? So try two or three. Start by simply making the first appointment.

If you still want to go to an allopathic MD, that's okay, but interview her or her staff before making the appointment. Is she open to alternative treatments? What does she think of the herb you're now taking? Is she willing to consult with your non-allopathic practitioner? What is her attitude about patients taking responsibility for their own health? How does she view her role in the healing process? Does she believe your condition can be cured? What role does she think attitude plays in healing? Ask anything that's important to you.

You interview before hiring an employee, why not before hiring a doctor? How much more important is your life than your business? The health-care practitioner—whether an MD or herbalist—works for you. Screen candidates to make sure you're hiring the right person for the job. If a practitioner or her staff won't answer your questions, move on to the next candidate.

Once you're at the health practitioner's office, what do you look for? How do you know if this person is any good?

First, listen to your intuitive right brain. Do you sense that he can help you? If you're not in the habit of paying attention to your gut feelings, that's okay. Just listen to your logical left brain. Does what the practitioner says about his treatment philosophy and methods make sense? It's less likely to work if you don't believe in it, so if you can't believe it, don't do it. If you think it's possible, try it.

Finally, see if it works. Isn't this the ultimate test? As long as it works, do you care how many double-blind studies have been done or who approves of the treatment? You want to get well. That's what matters. The practitioner can tell you how long it usually takes to notice the difference. And you will know soon enough whether it's working. If you can't tell by how you feel, you can have blood analyses and x-rays and other diagnostic tests done to find out if you're being cured.

Why do so many of us settle for a prognosis of, "There's nothing more that can be done?" There's always something more that can be done. If one thing doesn't work, why give up? Because your doctor tells you to? A doctor who tells you nothing more can be done has made you a helpless victim of biology gone awry.

Perhaps the most important question to ask when choosing any type of health-care practitioner is this: Does he put you in the relationship of victim/savior or of teacher/student?

Most MDs are taught that the patient is a victim of a mechanical body with a malfunctioning part, and without the doctor, it cannot be fixed. This type of practitioner doesn't bother to explain what went wrong or what he's going to do about it; you don't have the knowledge to understand it. He has to save you.

Holistic practitioners know that you're the one who heals yourself. They simply help put you on the right path and remove some of the blocks to healing. To do this, they have to share their knowledge, and perhaps interest you in adding your own knowledge to it. If they can accomplish the latter, they have given you...

Useful Tool 2: Knowledge

There's an old saying, "Knowledge is power." It's certainly true when it comes to healing yourself. If you're sick, you need to know what you're up against. It helps to know what caused your illness and how your illness works.

You also need to know all that's available to help you heal. You need to know what has worked for other people. What worked for the receptionist where you work? What worked for the Peruvian medicine man during the first millennium? What worked for the research biologist who lives next door and understands the science behind the cure?

This is called anecdotal evidence, and it's often discounted as unscientific. To try to bring you back to the fold, allopaths will tell you anecdotal evidence is worthless. Just remember this: You know that if you soak your tired, aching feet in hot water, they'll feel better. You know this not because of all the double-blind scientific studies you've read. You know it because it's what people experience.

On the other hand, MDs ignore the double-blind experiments that show non-monopoly substances are therapeutic. You'll recall that dozens of scientific studies by respected researchers have been done on urine and have shown its therapeutic applications. Yet how many doctors prescribe this free substance? Doctors do not prescribe substances that cannot be patented, because pharmaceutical companies can't profit from them. That doesn't mean they don't work.

So debunk the debunkers. Experiential knowledge is valid. If Tricia Bies put bloodroot on her tumor, and it caused her tumor to come out, it's true that bloodroot eliminated a tumor. When thousands of people have had the same experience of bloodroot eliminating a tumor, it's true for many people. That tells you it could become true for you.

The more information you have, the better you'll be able to help yourself. Tricia had learned only about the bloodroot paste but not about the healing salve that is supposed to be applied after the tumor comes off. Neither did she know that there are many other cancer salves that work more slowly but are gentler. Not a lot of information is available about these substances. The FDA tends to close companies that claim cures. But the information is available if you keep looking.

"Do your own research," says self-healer Andrew Yachad. "Don't rely on what the doctors tell you as gospel. People buy a house and want to know how everything in it works. Shouldn't you want to know how your body works?"

Gather as much information as you can from as many sources as possible. It reduces fear. It improves your safety margin in treating yourself. Information truly is power.

But all that information isn't going to help unless you take advantage of...

Useful Tool 3: Action

Once you've learned about all the things that have worked to heal others, try them.

Our cultural conditioning may create a fear reaction in you now. So it's time to think through this issue so you can understand why it's safe to try these things.

Medicinal herbs are safer than chemical drugs because they have built-in balancers. If one constituent in the herb is toxic, another will modify the toxicity. That doesn't mean you can just take any herb in any amount. However, if you choose to use one of the many that have been used safely for thousands of years and take the recommended dosage, you're relatively safe.

Another thing that makes taking herbs relatively safe is the fact that they're scrutinized so closely. The FDA's tolerance for injury from non-monopoly products is zero. One single report of a Rife machine injuring a user, and every Rife product will be off the market. One case of a woman becoming ill after drinking ten cups of comfrey tea in one sitting, and comfrey will no longer be available through commercial outlets. Very little that you find on a health-food store shelf has injured anyone. The minute it did, it would be pulled from every shelf in every health-food store in America.

Your prescription drug, on the other hand, has probably injured thousands of people. This is allowed. It's called side effects. It might kill a few hundred people before the FDA yanks it from the pharmacists' shelves.

Each year, there are 106,000 deaths from *properly administered* prescription drugs[1] and zero from properly administered herbs. So, which is safer: the chemical drugs the doctor prescribes or the natural substances your neighbor tells you about? Break through the illusion. Prescription drugs from the doctor are not safer than herbs recommended by a friend. Don't just take someone's word for it. Research it. Read the statistics. You'll discover that the safest course of action is to use natural substances. The medical monopoly wants you to think they're risky. That's not true. Think it through. Your life depends on it.

Once you've reasoned out that it's all right to try things that your doctor did not recommend, start trying them.

Do you have AIDS? Buy a Beck zapper. It costs less than two-hundred dollars and may work. Take goldenseal root; it's a great virus killer. Buy motivational tapes. Begin a spiritual quest. Eat a raw foods diet. Drink colloidal silver. None of these will harm you. One of them may cure you. If it doesn't, keep looking. Find other people who have cured their AIDS (yes, there are some). Ask them what they did. Try that.

Your doctor may tell you that full-blown AIDS is one-hundred percent fatal. Don't believe it. He simply has not been trained in the methods of cure. So you'll have to find them elsewhere. You'll have to experiment on yourself and be your own guinea pig.

If you cure yourself, others may say it was the placebo effect. Do you care? You used to be dying. Now you're living. So what if the cure was all in your head? The placebo effect is underrated. What's "all in your head" can cure. Why not use it?

So try everything: prayer, attitude adjustment, bioelectric and magnetic devices, therapeutic substances such as herbs and vitamins, therapeutic methods such as saunas and colonic irrigations, lifestyle changes such as eating organic foods and eliminating chemicals from your environment.

Try everything. And don't stop until something—or more likely, a combination of things—works. It may take two months to find, as with Victoria Boutenko's search for a cure. It may take four years, as with Kim Dunn's healing portfolio. But keep trying until you make it.

Along the way, you'll run into a few dead ends and wrong turns. You'll also run into a few things that help a little but are not the full solution. Don't stop. You're not done, but you've re-empowered yourself, and you're on the right path. It does lead back to health. And you can reach your destination.

Chapter 54

Illness isn't really healed until people discover its meaning and life purpose, until they see its role in their soul journey.
—Peter V. Madill,
an MD specializing in complex chronic illness in Sebastopol, Calif.

Transformations

Niro Markoff believes disease is a cry from the soul, a wake-up call, a motivator to positive change.

AIDS was her wake-up call. Because she listened to it, she is cured. The human immue deficiency virus is no longer in her blood.

Niro was infected by her lover, who had not known he was carrying the virus. He died from AIDS. When Niro tested positive for HIV in 1985 and was diagnosed with AIDS-related complex, she knew that she, too, faced a life-and-death struggle.

She did not let the fear and emotional pain of the diagnosis defeat her. Instead, she explored that fear and emotional pain. And in her journey to self-discovery, she found that her deep sense of unworthiness and her self-denial had so weakened her immune system that it was unable to fight the HIV virus. She delved deeply into her own mind and soul, searching out all things that led to imbalance and disease. She resolved to change those things. It was a difficult journey. By taking it, she learned to love herself, stand up for herself and set boundaries. And she discovered that by strengthening her spirit, she strengthened her body. By healing her soul, she healed her disease.

Six months after her initial diagnosis, a blood test came back negative for HIV antibodies.

"My heart exploded in joy! I knew it. My body had transcended the disease. I believe it was because I had learned the lesson of my disease, living from my true essence one moment at a time; therefore the teacher —the disease—could go away," Niro wrote in a book about her odyssey, *Why I Survive AIDS*.

Her doctors drew pint after pint of blood, searching vainly for the virus. They kept drawing more, unwilling to believe she had been cured. She never heard back from them.

"I guess I was naïve to have believed that the medical establishment would be open and willing to explore the alternative possibilities, which might assist them in finding a solution to the AIDS crisis," she wrote.

Although she doesn't claim to have the definitive cure for all disease, she found a piece of the puzzle. She discovered the connection between body, mind and spirit. And it transformed her.

"Although disease seems destructive to the physical level, it offers an opportunity to let go of everything that is false in us," she wrote. "The disease is the tool that keeps us awake and on our path toward our maximum potential."

For most of the self-healers in this book, the journey to recovery from disease included some kind of transformation. If you take responsibility for your healing, expect something to change. Perhaps it will be as simple as a change in diet or job. Perhaps it will be as large as adopting a new spiritual practice or life goal. But know that the journey usually includes some kind of change for the better. And this transformation can give meaning and purpose to the illness. It can make the difficult path back to health worthwhile.

For some self-healers, the transformation was religious or spiritual. Some, like Thomas Deer, started going to church again. Others, like Jacquie Compton, started going to church for the first time. Others, like Sharon Rosa, found a deep spiritual connection outside of organized religion.

Other transformations included simple lessons or small improvements in quality of life. Thomas Deer, for example, learned to slow down and appreciate life more. "It made me stop and smell the roses more. At this time of year, the woods are filled with wildflowers; you just appreciate them more," he says.

Sarah Clemente learned how to stand up to teenage peer pressure. "From my illness, I learned I can't let what other people think matter to me," she says.

Linda Pranzitelli learned a similar lesson through her illness. "I don't consider my worth to be determined by other people anymore," she says.

Darla Greenig said her illness gave her the gift of becoming less judgmental of others. "I came from a family of ten kids, and you didn't get sick. We came from sturdy stock. I didn't have a lot of compassion for other people who were sick," Darla says. "I think the gift is that I'm not as judgmental of other people and their problems. All I want to do is support them."

For many of the self-healers, recovering from chronic illness impacted them so much that it changed the direction of their entire lives. Their new life paths became helping others heal.

For Andrew Yachad, it meant teaching nutrition. For Sharon Rosa and Jacquie Compton, it meant becoming naturopathic physicians. Madhuri Cawley was already working in the healing profession, but she changed her specialization to natural hormone therapy and balancing the biochemistry of the body through nutrition. Jeff Houck learned Reiki and kinesiology. Linda Koep started a business selling the substances that cured her. Arlene Oostdyk and Annie Wilkin became distributors for Nature's Sunshine herbal products.

For Victoria Boutenko, the healing journey led to a new life for her entire family. The Boutenkos were so flabbergasted that they had cured such a wide variety of incurable diseases with something so simple as raw food, they have dedicated their lives to spreading the word.

Prior to their healings, the Boutenkos had owned several successful businesses, including one that sold Russian folk art and another than helped Russian businessmen receive training from U.S. experts. These businesses —and the resulting high income—suddenly became unimportant.

"We couldn't continue to do our previous businesses," Victoria recalls.

So they closed their businesses and started teaching about raw food. Now, they have written two books and spend their time traveling around the country giving seminars. "We wanted to let people know that they didn't have to suffer," Victoria says.

During the last several years of teaching a healthy diet, Victoria has learned that sick people aren't easy to reach. Don't be surprised about this. You'll be so excited about your healing, you'll want everyone to know that they, too, can be cured. What you'll find is that almost no one will listen. If you don't have the initials MD after your name, your advice will be ignored at best, ridiculed at worst. You'll watch friends and family members get sick, suffer, die, and you'll know it was unnecessary. If they only would have listened...

But remember, you too were once hypnotized into believing that you should only do what the doctor says. So go ahead and offer the information you learned on your healing journey, and be thankful for the one in ten or one in a hundred who uses it to heal.

After nearly three years of traveling throughout the nation teaching others, Victoria said her family has learned to give classes only to healthy people who want to stay healthy with a raw-food lifestyle.

"We learned not to tell sick people about raw foods. They're not our audience. They've bonded with their medical doctors and have so much fear. They're already brainwashed."

If you're still reading this book, you've begun to break free from the brainwashing. Don't stop. Get on the healing path. It leads in only one direction: to life.

Endnotes

Chapter 5

1. About one-third of all people whose hearts have stopped report that something happened after they died. About thirteen million adults in the United States are estimated to have had a near-death experience. It usually includes one or more of the following:
   • A feeling of leaving the body and hovering near the ceiling.
   • Sensations of movement through a dark space or tunnel.
   • Encountering a bright light that exudes love.
   • Meeting other people, often deceased relatives.
   • Reviewing your lifetime as it is replayed instantaneously and understanding how your actions affected other people.
   • Realizing that it's not yet time to die, so you must go back.
   For more information, visit the Web site of the International Association for Near-Death Studies at www.iands.org.

Chapter 17

1. Bernie S. Siegel, MD, *Love, Medicine and Miracles: Lessons Learned About Self-Healing from a Surgeon's Experience With Exceptional Patients*, copyright 1990, HarperCollins Publishers Inc.

Chapter 21

1. Ivan Illich, *Medical Nemesis*, Random House, 1976.

2. Daniel Haley, *Politics in Healing: The Suppression and Manipulation of American Medicine*, Potomac Valley Press, 2000.

3. Gideon Bosker, *Pills That Work, Pills That Don't: Demanding and Getting the Best and Safest Medications for Your Family,* Random House, 1997.

4. Ellen Hodgson Brown and Lynn Paige Walker, *The Informed Consumer's Pharmacy: The Essential Guide to Prescription and Over-The-Counter Drugs*, Carroll & Graf, 1991.

Chapter 29

1. *World Without Cancer* may be ordered from www.realityzone.com or by calling 1-800-595-6596.

Chapter 30

1. Kathy's web site is at www.5pillars.com/atlast/

Chapter 32

1. *Science News*, March 30, 1991, page 207.

Chapter 36

1. Conducted by the Picker Institute of Boston, Mass., in conjunction with the American Hospital Association.

2. Reported in a 1999 study of baby boomers commissioned by Triad Healthcare, Inc., and conducted by Sorelli B, an independent national research firm specializing in healthcare.

3. Richard A. Cooper, MD, and Sandi Stoflet, "Trends in the Education and Practice of Alternative Medicine Clinicians," *Health Affairs* 15:3, Fall 1996, pages 226-238.

4. Eisenberg, D.M.; Kessler, R.C.; Foster. C.; Norlock F.E.; Calkins D.R.; Delbanco, T.L. "Unconventional Medicine in the United States," *New England Journal of Medicine* 1993:328, pages 246-52.

5. "Trends in Alternative Medicine Use in the United States," *Journal of the American Medical Association*, Jan. 11, 1998.

Chapter 47

1. Sergei also began exercising and now runs at least four miles almost every day. Victoria believes this is imperative for a diabetic, because exercised muscles produce insulin. "I'm not sure that raw food alone would work" for diabetes, she says. A good resource for diabetics is Dr. Julian M. Whitaker's book, *Reversing Diabetes: Reduce or Even Eliminate Your Dependence on Insulin or Oral Drugs*.

Chapter 53

1. *Journal of the American Medical Association*, April 15, 1998.

Bibliography

Bach, Edward. *Heal Thyself*. Oxfordshire, England: The Dr. Edward Bach Healing Centre, 1931.

Baroody, Theodore A. *Alkalize or Die: Superior Health Through Proper Alkaline-Acid Balance*. Waynesville, N.C.: Eclectic Press, 1991.

Beasley, Joseph D. *The Betrayal of Health: The Impact of Nutrition, Environment, and Lifestyle on Illness in America*. New York: Times Books, 1991.

Becker, Robert O. *Cross Currents: The Promise of Electromedicine, the Perils of Electropollution*. Los Angeles: J.P. Tarcher, 1991.

Berger, Stuart M. *What Your Doctor Didn't Learn in Medical School... And What You Can Do About It*. New York: William Morrow and Company, 1988.

Bosker, Gideon. *Pills That Work, Pills That Don't: Demanding and Getting the Best and Safest Medications for You and Your Family*. New York: Random House/Fawcett, 1998.

Boutenko, Victoria. *12 Steps to Raw Foods: How to End Your Addiction to Cooked Food*. Ashland, Ore.: Raw Family Publishing, 2001.

Brown, Ellen Hodgson, and Walker, Lynn Paige. *Informed Consumer's Pharmacy: The Essential Guide to Prescription and Over-the-Counter Drugs*. New York: Carroll & Graf, 1991.

Capra, Fritjof. *The Turning Point: Science, Society and the Rising Culture*. New York: Simon & Schuster, 1981.

Chappell, Terry, and Whitaker, Julian. *Questions from the Heart: Answers to 100 Questions About Chelation Therapy, a Safe Alternative to Bypass Surgery.* Charlottesville, Va.: Hampton Roads, 1996.

Chopra, Deepak. *Quantum Healing: Exploring the Frontiers of Mind Body Medicine.* New York: Bantam Books, 1990.

Christy, Martha M. *Your Own Perfect Medicine: The Incredible Proven Natural Miracle Cure That Medical Science Has Never Revealed.* Tempe, Ariz.: Self-Healing Press, 1994.

Clark, Hulda R. *The Cure for All Diseases.* San Diego, Calif.: New Century Press, 1995.

Diamond, John. *Your Body Doesn't Lie: How to Increase Your Life Energy Through Behavioral Kinesiology.* New York: Harper & Rowe, 1979.

Dubos, René Jules. *Man, Medicine, and Environment.* New York: Frederick A. Praeger; 1968.

Feuer, Elaine. *Innocent Casualties: The FDA's War Against Humanity.* Pittsburgh, Penn.: Dorrance Publishing Co., 1998.

Goodman, Jordan, and Walsh, Vivien. *The Story of Taxol: Nature and Politics in the Pursuit of an Anti-Cancer Drug.* Cambridge, Mass.: Cambridge University Press, 2001.

Gordon, James S. *Manifesto for a New Medicine: Your Guide to Healing Partnerships and the Wise Use of Alternative Therapies.* New York: Perseus Books, 1997.

Griffin, G. Edward. *World Without Cancer: The Story of Vitamin B17.* American Media, 1997.

Hahnemann, Samual. *Organon of Medicine*. Los Angeles: J.P. Tarcher, 1982.

Haley, Daniel. *Politics in Healing: The Suppression & Manipulation of American Medicine*. Washington D.C.: Potomac Valley Press, 2001.

Illich, Ivan. *Medical Nemesis: The Expropriation of Health*. New York: Random House/Pantheon, 1976.

Jensen, Bernard. *Dr. Jensen's Guide to Better Bowel Care: A Complete Program for Tissue Cleansing Through Bowel Management*. New York: Avery Penguin Putnam, 1998.

Justice, Blair. *Who Gets Sick: How Beliefs, Moods and Thoughts Affect Health*. Houston, Texas: Peak Press, 2000.

Knowles, John H. *Doing Better and Feeling Worse: Health in the United States*. New York: W.W. Norton & Company, 1977.

Leviton, Richard. *Physician: Medicine and the Unsuspected Battle for Human Freedom*. Charlottesville, Va.: Hampton Roads, 2000.

Lisa, Joseph. *The Assault on Medical Freedom*. Charlottesville, Va.: Hampton Roads, 1994.

Olsen, Cynthia. *Essiac: A Native Herbal Cancer Remedy*. Pagosa Springs, Colo.: Kali Press, 1998.

Markoff, Niro. *Why I Survive AIDS*. New York: Simon & Schuster/Fireside, 1991.

Mowrey, Daniel B. *The Scientific Validation of Herbal Medicine*. New York: McGraw-Hill, 1986.

Naiman, Ingrid. *Cancer Salves: A Botanical Approach to Treatment*. Santa Fe, N.M.: Seventh Ray Press, 1999.

Ruwart, Mary. *Healing Our World: The Other Piece of the Puzzle.* Kalamazoo, Mich.: SunStar Press, 1992.

Schneider, Robert G. *When to Say No to Surgery: How to Evaluate the Most Often Performed Operations.* New York: Prentice Hall, 1982.

Siegel, Bernie S. *Love, Medicine and Miracles: Lessons Learned About Self-Healing from a Surgeon's Experience With Exceptional Patients.* New York: Harper Perennial, 1990.

Talman, Donna H., and Briggs, William A. *Heartsearch: Toward Healing Lupus.* Berkeley, Calif.: North Atlantic Books, 1991.

Trevino, Haven, et al. *The Tao of Healing: Meditations for Body and Spirit.* Novato, Calif.: New World Library, 1999.

Wolfe, Sidney M. *Pills That Don't Work: A Consumers' and Doctors' Guide to 610 Prescription Drugs That Lack Evidence of Effectiveness.* New York: Farrar, Straus & Giroux, 1981.

Winters, Jason. *In Search of the Perfect Cleanse.* Las Vegas, Nev.: Vinton Publishing Co., 1986.

Wolper, Sally. *Tijuana Clinics: Alternative Therapies—Hospitals & Medical Centers—Where and How to Go.* San Diego, Calif.: Promotion Publishing, 1995.

Index

82, 84, 126, 141, 142, 147,
150, 159, 160, 212, 214,
226, 232, 233, 241, 248,
253, 254, 255, 263
naturopathic 32, 43, 52, 77, 79,
82, 84, 126, 150, 212, 226,
254, 263
near-death experience 31, 32, 267
nerves 26, 44, 166, 232
New England Journal of Medicine
161, 269
Newton, Isaac 66, 169
Nobel Prize 132, 228
nutrition 37, 68, 70, 76, 83, 103,
134, 145, 182, 185, 196,
200, 201, 205, 213, 215,
224, 235, 240, 255, 263
nystatin 180, 181, 200, 241

O

Oostdyk, Arlene 69, 70, 95, 142,
263

P

pain 12, 13, 23, 27, 32, 33, 34,
44, 45, 48, 51, 57, 59, 61,
76, 78, 82, 92, 119, 134,
135, 140, 141, 145, 155,
167, 186, 189, 192, 196,
199, 200, 225, 228, 233,
234, 236, 237, 238, 240,
241, 261
pancreas 35, 73, 97, 219
parasites 147, 211, 212, 214, 232
Pauling, Linus 129, 132
pelvic inflammatory disease 134
pesticides 41, 72, 112, 205, 209,
212, 213, 224, 225
phantom diseases 98
pharmaceuticals 48, 96, 106, 129—
136, 138, 139, 142, 145,

162, 257
Pharmaceutical Manufacturers
Association 116
plague 102, 103
pneumonia 43, 216
polarity therapy 37, 254
Popular Health Movement 106
Pranzitelli, Linda 51—52, 83, 241—
242, 262
prayer 51, 89, 246—247, 259
prescriptions 26, 81, 82, 93, 96,
97, 109, 122, 131, 137, 138,
153, 200, 206, 207, 208,
214, 216, 255, 258, 259,
preventive medicine 67, 158
probability theory 170
prostate cancer 62, 155
Public Citizens Health Research Group
127
Pure Food and Drug Act 130

Q

Qigong 169, 172, 213—214
quantum physics 150, 151, 167—
172
quassia root 241

R

radiation therapy 49, 50, 60, 91,
95, 120, 155, 156
raw food 196, 213, 220—222, 259,
263, 264
red clover 92
reductionism 64, 67, 111, 165,
166, 167, 172
reflexology 254
Reiki 169, 172, 254, 263
renal cell cancer 49
research 15, 29, 37, 45, 48, 62,
63, 65, 66, 71, 72, 75, 76,
81, 87, 88, 91, 92, 95, 101,

Y

Yachad, Andrew 29, 62, 77, 81,
141, 155, 215—216, 258, 263
yellow dock 232

Z

zapper 145—147, 172, 214, 224,
225, 228, 238, 259

About the Author

Teresa Tsalaky is a newspaper publisher who lives on California's redwood coast. Listed in Who's Who in the West, she has won numerous awards for her writing and editing.

Special Offer

If you're a health-care practitioner who wants to help patients help themselves, you can take 40 percent off the cover price of *To Life: A Guide to Finding Your Path Back to Health* when you order five or more copies.

Spread the word that your healing system is valid and effective.

To order, go to www.tolifeone.com, click on "Bookstore," and print the Mail Order Form, or call toll-free, 1-877-371-5017.

Notes